In Over
Your Head

SUSIE LARSON

In Over Your Head

HARVEST HOUSE PUBLISHERS
EUGENE, OREGON

Cover by Emily Weigel

Cover Image © Y Photo Studio, hfng, therealtakeone / Shutterstock

Published in association with the literary agency of Alive Communications, Inc., 7680 Goddard Street, Ste. #200, Colorado Springs, CO 80920. www.aliveliterary.com

Every effort has been made to ensure that the information contained in this book is complete and accurate. However, neither the author nor the publisher is engaged in rendering professional advice or services to the reader, individually or in groups. The ideas and suggestions contained in this book are not intended as substitutes for consulting professionals, as appropriate. Accordingly, individual readers and groups must assume responsibility for their own actions, safety, and health, and neither the author nor the publisher shall be liable or responsible for any loss, injury, or damage allegedly arising from any information or suggestion in this book.

Every effort has been made to give proper credit for all stories, poems, and quotations. If for any reason proper credit has not been given, please notify the author or publisher, and proper notation will be given in future printings.

IN OVER YOUR HEAD

Previously published as *Balance That Works When Life Doesn't*
Copyright © 2005/2018 by Susie Larson
Published by Harvest House Publishers
Eugene, Oregon 97408
www.harvesthousepublishers.com

ISBN 978-0-7369-7375-5 (pbk.)
ISBN 978-0-7369-7376-2 (eBook)

The Library of Congress has cataloged the earlier printing as follows:

Larson, Susie, 1962-
    Balance that works when life doesn't / Susie Larson.
        p. cm.
    ISBN 978-0-7369-1642-4
    1. Christian women—Religious life. 2. Time management—Religious aspects—Christianity.
    I. Title.
BV4527.L37 2005
248.8′43—dc22   2005001899

Printed in the United States of America

18 19 20 21 22 23 24 25 26 / VP-GL / 10 9 8 7 6 5 4 3 2 1

To Kevin
*Your earnest commitment to guard our margin, to pray big
prayers, and to pursue a life of balance is a continual source of
healing, joy, and strength in my life. Thank you, honey.
I'll love you forever.*

*To Jesus,
How can I ever thank You enough for
Your redeeming work in my life?
I love You so much.
I'll follow You forever.*

Contents

How to Use This Book

Look back over seasons when you found yourself feeling irritable, frustrated, tired, and out of whack. Consider that maybe—a little at a time—you let go of what you knew was good for you, and you filled your time with what cost you but didn't nourish you for the long run.

I've learned that if we're willing to put even a few hours a week into our physical and spiritual health, that discipline will carry us a long way. And we'll walk in an accumulative strength as a result. When we live a hit-and-miss lifestyle with something so important as our physical and spiritual health, we'll never quite hit our stride or enjoy the kind of life-rhythm God has for us.

If you're ready to incorporate some healthy habits with dividends, let's do this! Remember, you don't have to apply every idea in this book. I suggest you don't. Instead, as you prayerfully work through its pages, trust God to quicken your heart and speak to you about your next right choices. Ask Him to give you the grace and the "want-to" to stick with healthy habits and make them a normal part of your life.

The amazing thing is you could read this book again next year, be in a whole new place, and realize you're ready for more healthy habits. Give yourself grace, but also be willing to give yourself a little push. You know what you can handle, and Jesus cares deeply for you. He'll be with you every step of the way.

Each chapter concludes with the following components:

- *Prayer*—To encourage you
- *Steps Toward Health*—Say these out loud, because faith comes by hearing (Romans 10:17), and when you hear yourself declare these truths and healthy determinations, it'll play a part in changing your mind-set and gaining a whole new momentum.

- *Try This*—Here you'll find advice on some potential next steps. Pick the ones that resonate with you and will work for you.

- *Balance Application*—This section summarizes the chapter, boiling it down for you. Hopefully these truths will begin to make a deep impact on your soul.

- *Study Time*—For those who want to take a deeper dive into Scripture, I've provided a handful of verses to look up and some questions to ponder. You'll need a journal or a notebook for this exercise. (Note: It'd be great if you wrote down some of your goals and expectations at the front of the journal and kept them before you daily. Remember, this isn't a fad diet or a once-and-done sort of thing. This is all about a lifestyle change so you can last long and finish strong.)

- *Personal Reflection*—I'd love to see you commit to working your way through these questions. I ask you to do some real soul-searching, and I think you're ready for it! Your journal is a great place to record your thoughts, prayers, and answers to these questions.

- *This Week's Goal*—Use this section to write down even the simplest goal. For example, *My goal is to quit the negative, berating self-talk.* Or, *My goal is to quit eating sweets during the week.* You get the idea. On one hand, be kind to yourself (don't set impossible goals and then beat yourself up for falling short), but on the other hand, remember that growth and forward progress always costs us something. Be willing to ask something of yourself. God is working in you, helping you to do what's good, and right, and true.

- *God's Promise to Me*—This section is also optional, but I think it's an important, powerful exercise. Based on your overall personal goals (or even your goal for that week), find a Bible promise to pray about and memorize. For instance, if you're constantly tempted to eat more than you should, write down 1 Corinthians 10:13 and own that promise. I've made the most strides in my Christian journey through knowing, praying, and standing on the promises of God.

See this journey not as an obligation to shape up, but as an invitation to step up.

I'll be praying for you. And I'm proud of you.

Do You Ever Wonder?

I wonder why we wander from what nourishes our souls. We wander from healthy eating, right thinking, and time with God. We wander from faithful friends, quality time, and the challenge to grow deeper. We lose the fight for what's best for us when we don't fight at all. Somehow, for some reason, our steps take us from our appointed road toward a less-than-best path for us. Do we really enjoy living a peripheral life? I don't think so. Is it easier? Perhaps it's more convenient, but I don't think it's easier. Living a life of second bests and stuck places wears on our soul and steals our joy.

On the other hand, in the moments when things line up for us, when we are doing what we care about, passion emerges and joy returns. We find ourselves wondering, *Why did I ever let this go?* And yet we do let it go—over and over again.

Is it that we don't care enough? I think we care a lot. But our priorities get skewed because we live in a fallen world where the currents of sin and defeat are strong, and if not resisted, will pull us under. *That's* when we feel in over our head. And that's when we feel at the mercy of our crazy lives. As long as we walk this earth, we will contend with the current. But this shouldn't shake us, because God has made a way for us. We're not at the mercy of our schedules, our culture, or even our weaknesses. *We're in the mercy of God,* which eclipses every lesser thing around us. Even our weaknesses become a thing of beauty and strength when we're hidden in Christ Jesus.

God is immovable; we are the ones who move. God is consistent; we have our moments. God is powerful; we are powerless without Him. All His thoughts are pure and holy; ours can be selfish and small. We need Jesus. Just as we need oxygen to breathe, we continually need

Jesus's input, His breath, and His Spirit in and through us. He is our Source. We must stay close to the Source.

Given that backdrop, how are you today? Read through the following questions:

1. Do you wish you had more energy?
2. Do you lack focus, passion, and direction?
3. Do you feel at the mercy of your schedule? Is life pulling you in too many directions?
4. Does the term "spiritual health" make you think of rigid rules and an *un-maintainable* level of holiness?
5. Would you like to be more physically fit?
6. Would you like to enjoy a greater awareness of God's love for you?

If you answered yes to any of these questions, join me as we explore the wonder of our physical and spiritual health. God has divinely woven them together. You must know at the outset that you are loved and accepted right where you are. But if you are interested, God has more for you!

If you're tired of halfhearted living, this book can help. Get ready to take a fearless inventory of your habits and choices. As you read, ask God to lead you out of the swirling current of imbalance to a place of stability and strength in both your physical and spiritual life.

You'll begin to feel relieved as you find yourself "off the hook" from having to achieve a certain picture of perfection. On the other hand, you'll feel "back on the hook" as you are challenged in every circumstance to find the most fruitful place amid your life's current season.

This book has two parts—physical health and spiritual health—and both will deal with essential components of health and holiness. At the end of each chapter, you'll find study and reflection questions for both individual and group use. Take your time and pray through every chapter. Allow God to speak to you, deal with you, heal you, and set you free to powerfully affect the world around you. When you are at your best, the world around you is blessed!

My prayer is that, as you read, you'll accept God's forgiveness and leave your past behind. May you trust Jesus with your future so you'll be fully alive in the *present moment*. May your soul be awakened to all you have in Him today. May you be a living, breathing example of Christ's love for a lost world, so when others encounter you, they encounter Him.

Bless the day, my sister!

Susie Larson

Part One

Physical Health

I discipline my body like an athlete,
training it to do what it should.
Otherwise, I fear that after preaching to others
I myself might be disqualified.
1 Corinthians 9:27

One

How Did I Get Here?

*Then Jesus said, "Come to me, all of you who are weary
and carry heavy burdens, and I will give you rest. Take my
yoke upon you. Let me teach you, because I am humble
and gentle at heart, and you will find rest for your souls. For
my yoke is easy to bear, and the burden I give you is light."*
MATTHEW 11:28-30

My good intentions had gotten the best of me. I said yes to far too many opportunities, and now I was paying a costly price. I had no room in my life for red lights, wide-load trucks, or leaky dishwashers. Every minute had its place in my day as I whipped from one task to another, checking them off my list upon completion.

As my car sped around a bend, I chomped on a dry bagel. The trees went by in a blur. The thought *Savor the flavor* crossed my mind, but I waved it away as though it were a gnat circling my head. I made it to the bank, the library, and then reached the restaurant just in time for my lunch appointment. How did I end up on this fast track again? Where did that place of peace go? I shoveled down a salad as I listened intently to my friend. *Savor.* There it was again. My friend and I shared a wonderful time, but it was over before I knew it.

A glance at my watch reminded me I still had three stops to make before heading home in time to meet the kids as they got off the bus.

My friend and I embraced and promised not to let so much time pass before we met again. The gurgle sounds coming from my stomach made me realize that perhaps I had eaten a bit too fast. *Savor the flavor.*

I marched out to my car and got behind the wheel. I turned the key, revved the engine, and then took my foot off the gas pedal. I listened to the steady hum of the motor and marveled at the irony. The engine didn't drive itself; *I* was the one with the lead foot. And nobody pushed me to keep such a fast pace in life; my own drive pushed me.

I paused and prayed, *What is it You're trying to tell me, Lord?* I sensed His whisper in return: *You are living in the "next" moment and missing the present one. You are so focused on your destination that you're simply consumed with getting there. Did you happen to notice the beautiful sky I painted this morning? How about the trees? Did you notice how the treetops were blanketed with fresh snow? Take your salad today; you were so busy stabbing your next bite that you were totally unaware of the great morsel of food you already had in your mouth. That taste was history before it ever hit your lips. Wouldn't it be wonderful to savor the flavor of the bite in your mouth? Be thankful for the abundance of food in front of you and take a moment to enjoy it. You're missing so much of the journey because your mind is on the destination.*

I wasn't sure how long I sat there, but it didn't matter. My life needed some tweaking, and Jesus had just spiritually adjusted me. My life had subtly shifted out of whack to the point that I'd completely overlooked the significant gifts He'd sent my way throughout the day.

I decided my other errands could wait, and I headed home. On the way I pulled back on the gas pedal and slowed way down as I rounded that same bend. I looked at the lofty pines that pointed to the heavens. I even put the window down several inches just to breathe in the crisp winter air. "Thank You, Jesus, for this beautiful day."

I arrived home in time to see my kids get off the bus. Instead of rushing to get that one extra load of dishes done before they burst through the door, I went to the living room window and watched them as they hoofed through the deep snow with rosy cheeks and thick winter garb. They lobbed a few snowballs across the street to their neighbor buddies and then ducked behind a snow mound to dodge returning fire. They grow up so fast. I breathed a prayer:

Help me to make the best of these days, Lord. Help me not to race through each one. I want to see the miracles in front of me. May I remember that each day is a special gift, wrapped in a supernatural bow. Oh, and by the way, thank You for that beautiful sky. It's going to be a glorious sunset.

> "Help me to make the best of these days, Lord. Help me not to race through each one. I want to see the miracles in front of me."

As I watched my kids make their way to the front door, my mind wandered back to a tougher time in our lives. We were on the cancer floor of the hospital with our little boy. He was having night sweats and had a large lump on his neck. We watched as they wheeled him away for various tests. But something was different during this trial. Because of the many crises we'd endured in previous years, we finally believed God to be who He said He was. We truly knew God was for us (Romans 8:31). We could take Him at His word, and we did. Even though we were nervous and on edge, we had an inner peace and stability.

We also had many people praying for us, visiting us, and taking care of our household duties. We received great blessings from family, our church, and the hospital. I felt so cared for that, even in the middle of our crisis, I had something to give away. I sat in a large rocking chair and watched all the precious, hairless children welcome my child into the fold. I found myself asking, *What does obedience look like here, Lord? How can I love, serve, and obey You in this setting?* The Lord whispered to my heart, *Watch the other moms and dads. Look at the fatigue in their eyes and pray for them. They live this every day. Listen to them and help to carry their load.* I looked around at some of the world's greatest unsung heroes.

Life moves so fast. We have appointments, luncheons, hockey games, videos, late fees, highways, skyways, hallways, and *my way*. Here it was just the opposite: aches, pains, prayers, tears, hallways, dark ways, lost ways, slow days, and not my way. Wow. Nobody looked polished around here. They looked tired and weary. They didn't seem to notice, because this was not their focus; their children were.

I lost track of time as they shared their stories. I was thankful to have the opportunity to pray for a weary grandmother and grateful to receive comfort from her as well. I had an underlying strength that held fast. This was a powerful revelation to me—I found the eye of the storm, the axis in a very stressful situation. I saw myself fully as a child of God. I was under His care, but I was also under His charge. And since I had strength to give, He provided the opportunity to serve.

Somehow, I had found my place of balance in that crisis (thankfully, our son *didn't* have cancer). And yet here in this place and time, watching my healthy boys get off the bus, I realized that by overcommitting myself, I gave too much away, and with it, my sense of wonder. God called me back once again, to find my peace with Him in the season I was in.

Balance Is More Than Skin Deep

Now, granted, in times of crisis we need to receive far more than we're capable of giving. We also experience times of strength and grace when we can give much more than we're receiving. But we cannot for too long give at the expense of receiving without losing our health and perspective. And we must never let go of the fact that we are living, breathing creatures made for a heavenly kingdom. God always provides nourishment for our souls; He also sets up many divine appointments where we can offer a blessing, and He paints many beautiful skies that call us to lie down and look up.

True balance isn't defined by the appearance of having it all together. Some of the most together-looking women are the most out of balance—at least from a heavenly point of view. In the worldly sense, self-realization and self-ambition have become celebrated idols. Promoting ourselves, our gifts, and our abilities is an expected and acceptable road in the secular arena. But as women of faith who love our Savior, we are called to a much different path. He is the point, He is the One who gets the credit, and He is the One we serve.

The irony is that as we embrace the God-given components of a healthy life, we *will* look more put together. We will *have* more together. But this won't be our highest aim, because we know better than anyone how quickly life can change. Our goal and our aim is to pursue the mind-set that we are *alive* in Christ. He wants to breathe life into us so we can serve Him by living a healthy, holy, and abundant life. Scripture promises we will encounter trials and troubles. Yet we are also promised access to the very power that raised Christ from the dead (Ephesians 1:19-20).

Since Christ has paid for and provided for every scenario, we have all we need to embrace life with a sense of purpose, power, and balance. This kind of balance goes with us and adjusts to the places God takes us and to whatever He allows to happen in our lives.

Balance Is Worth Pursuing

Where are you right now? It doesn't matter if your road is rough or smooth; there is balance to be found and greater health to be realized. Even in the valley, there is higher ground—the place of greatest fruitfulness—and it is *that* place we seek in every situation. As we move along in our journey toward balance, you will receive practical tips to help you both physically and spiritually. You will be challenged to go just a bit further than you may feel like going. If you apply the principles in this book, you will get healthier, but more importantly, you will begin to see yourself as Christ sees you. Your perspective will change. Your tastes will change. And before you know it, you'll lose your taste for what weakens you, and you'll more consistently hunger and thirst for what nourishes you both physically and spiritually. I pray this book will help you find your place with Jesus no matter where life finds you.

Father God,

You have done so much for me, and I thank You with all my heart. I don't know why I sometimes choose the less-than-best path when I know there is a better way. Motivate me to start anew today. Help me to find my way to the peace You provide. I want to take what You have given and give You a great return on Your investment. Create in me an excitement to live a healthier life. I love You. In Jesus's mighty name, I pray, amen.

Steps Toward Health

- If my life is currently caught in the swirling current, I will come before God today and find my place of peace with Him. I will ask Him to show me what needs to go from my schedule.

- If my life is currently a peaceful, balanced place, I will thank God today for blessing me in this way. I will ask the Lord to show me practical ways to guard the balance I'm enjoying right now while looking for opportunities to stretch, grow, and be a blessing to the world around me.

- I will be mindful of the fine line between a healthy protection of my balance and a selfish protection of my personal comforts. I will ask the Lord to heighten my conviction so I will instantly notice when I begin to approach the "selfish line."

- I will ask the Lord to prepare me to take this journey toward health and holiness. I will stand in faith, knowing He will come through for me.

- I will prayerfully consider the idea that God has someone in mind right now, someone with whom I'm supposed to take this journey, someone I can bless and encourage and who will do the same for me.

Try This

- If you feel hopelessly overcommitted while looking at this month's calendar, sit down and pray. Ask the Lord to show you what can be rescheduled or taken off your schedule. Make the phone calls and the necessary adjustments.

- Look at your calendar and "X" off a day or two each week when you plan not to have plans, especially those days that fall right before or right after an event or a commitment that may deplete you.

- Write down a list of five high-priority items you want to accomplish this month (for example, go on a date with your child, catch up on paperwork, visit a grandparent). Post that short list next to your monthly calendar. When you receive calls and requests for commitments, measure those requests against what you felt convicted to accomplish at the beginning of your month. Guard your time, and accomplish what you know you should.

Balance Application

If life is too busy, make the adjustments necessary to find your place of peace again. If you are in a crisis, whether or not it feels natural, seek after God and find your place with Him so you are not swept away with your fears. Some crises are so intense that the Lord Himself carries us through without any pressing in on our part. If you are on a smooth path, guard it and look for ways to be a blessing to others.

Study Time

1. Read Ruth 2:8-22.

2. Do you see a parallel between Boaz's care for Ruth and your heavenly Father's care for you? Explain.

3. In what tangible ways did Boaz equip and care for Ruth?

4. Why was it important for Ruth to stay within the boundaries set for her?

5. Why is it important for you to do the same?

6. Ruth was a woman of honor, diligence, humility, and gratitude. In what ways do you see God establishing these virtues in you?

7. Pause and pray. Ask the Lord to draw you closer to Him.

Personal Reflection

1. In what ways have you missed God's provision and goodness because of your current pace? Write out a prayer and express your thoughts to Him.

2. Someone once asked, "If I woke up tomorrow with only what I thanked God for today, what would I still possess?" Spend some extended time surveying your life, and count every blessing you'd miss tomorrow if it went away.

3. Given the current immovables in your life (what you cannot change), what would a life of rhythm and balance look like for you? Spend some time with Jesus. Ask Him for a fresh vision for this season of life and for wisdom and clarity around your next steps.

This Week's Goal:

_____

_____

_____

God's Promise to Me:

_____

_____

_____

What Keeps You Balanced, Grounded?

I think when it comes to balancing out my life, I've found that I need to go to the Living Water that gives life first. I need to stop the comparison game and I need to listen to God's calling on my life, because when I listen to God and hear Him speak, then He is the one who balances out all the details.

Life can be a beautiful, messy balance, but God loves when the mess is blessed by Him.

—Heather

Two

What Balance Isn't

*There has never been the slightest doubt in my
mind that the God who started this great work in
you would keep at it and bring it to a flourishing
finish on the very day Christ Jesus appears.*

PHILIPPIANS 1:6 MSG

I tried to rest, but I couldn't. The pain kept me from falling into a deep sleep. I looked once more at the needle pokes up and down my arms and sighed. My veins kept collapsing, requiring new sites for the IV. I stared at the plastic cylinder imbedded in my arm. Attached to it was a long tube that reached up to a bag of medicine, which hung on the mini-blinds behind the couch. This medicine was a mixed bag of blessings and curses. On the one hand, the fluid offered my only hope for recovery. On the other hand, it cost us a fortune, which forced us deeper into debt. The medicine made me sick, weak, and tired, but it was also supposed to make me better—to give me back my life.

Whenever I think back to that time—when I was battling Lyme disease—I remember clearly how the battle affected me on several fronts: physically, spiritually, and emotionally. Vertigo, joint pain, scary neurological symptoms, and mind-bending fatigue had their way with me. The Enemy also seemed to have unhindered access to me. (I later learned he's on a short leash, but it certainly didn't feel true then.) Fear, anxiety, and worry confronted me daily. Our finances seemed broken beyond repair, and my twenty-something body felt the same way.

My life never looked as imbalanced as it did back then. Rather than teaching group fitness classes, my extra exertion came in the form of taking a shower—once a week. More than that, it drained from me any energy I possessed. Our house needed repair, our debt took on a life of its own, and our friends wearied themselves as they chipped in to care for our three little boys because I was too sick to do so.

So yes, when I look back, I remember what a tough season that was for us. But I'm also thankful for the treasures I gained. In that terrible valley I learned surrender, brokenness, and trust. I had to reckon with the promise I'd made long ago when I gave my life to Jesus. Was I serious about my commitment to Him when it seemed He was answering none of my prayers? After many sleepless nights, fist-pounding laments, and fear-filled tears, I decided I *was* serious about my heart's cry for more of Him and less of me.

The hardest part for me was my inability to produce *anything*. In fact, just the opposite occurred. I was costing money, time, resources, and energy, and I could do nothing about it. For a "doer," this was a nightmare come true. And yet only in my depletion could I have found God to be my *everything*. As I faced the black hole of insecurity that hid beneath all my efforts, I found that God's love fills every empty place (when we're not filling them with something else). He *is* the Source of identity, of hope, and of life itself. Had I not plummeted to the depths of despair and sickness, I would not have been able to grasp the scope of His love and care for His people.

We live in a society that measures value by what we produce and how many titles we claim. But we cannot and must not allow such a shallow measure to define what God has created. Although from the outside I looked as though I was wasting away—costing much, contributing little—that valley provided my life's highest education.

Because God went to great lengths to create in you something that has never been done before nor ever will be again, you must let *Him* decide your worth. He knows best how you are wired, so allow *Him* to become your point of reference—the filter through which you run every thought, every circumstance, and every opportunity; every fear, insecurity, and worry; every season, every storm, and every blessing. You were made by Him and for Him. You can trust Him to establish you. (We'll look at this in depth later.)

> Because God went to great lengths to create in you something that has never been done before or ever will be again, you must let Him decide your worth.

"Our lives are a Christ-like fragrance rising up to God. But this fragrance is perceived differently by those who are being saved and by those who are perishing" (2 Corinthians 2:15). We measure our lives by a different standard because our highest goal is not to be admired and accepted by the world, but to live free and full lives that honor God and bless others.

Before we can maintain a godly balance in our lives, we must first define what balance isn't.

Balance Is Not...A Put-Together Appearance

Women who appear extremely put together can sometimes be the most imbalanced of persons. When emphasis is placed on perfecting outward presentation, it can be at the expense of true personal growth. Women who work too hard to appear perfectly together tell me they do so because another area in their lives feels completely out of control.

Some women, however, just have a knack for keeping it all together—God bless 'em. I sometimes think one reason they were put on this earth is to keep the rest of us humbly dependent on Jesus. There is a wonderful consolation here, though. As you pursue a life of godly balance and health, you will *look* more together and you will *have* more together. But this should not be our goal. Being fully alive in Christ is our goal. As we gain ground both physically and spiritually, we will hold what we love with an open hand, fully trusting Jesus's work in our lives. The pursuit of God with a posture of trust keeps us positioned and prepared for all that comes our way.

Balance Is Not...A Perfectly Managed Schedule

We can't get around the need for calendars, smartphones, and list apps. Because of our multifaceted life, we need to stay on top of our tasks and commitments lest we be completely overwhelmed by the rat-race culture of our day. And the truth is, some women are just good at this stuff. They are punctual, perfect managers of their appointments, arrivals, and departures. And there's great virtue in being organized and prompt. I once heard someone say, "Being late is a form of selfishness; I'm basically saying I care more about my schedule than I do about yours." Ouch. Very true.

To be frantic, harried, and forgetful of where we are supposed to be and when we're supposed to be there certainly undermines our witness. However, balance is not simply a perfectly managed schedule. In fact, some of the best schedule managers I have ever seen forget about little things, like, say...people! Far too many people spend more time with their smartphones than the people right in front of them. How many sunsets, smiles, and tasty morsels have we missed because we're mind-lessly swiping through our phones? When it is all said and done, people and God are what will last, and if we spend our days serving and mastering our schedules, we'll miss the needs of those around us. When this happens, we lose, and those we were appointed to touch lose as well.

While managing our schedules is a component to balance, true balance also has a flexibility and adaptability to it. True balance makes the plan but allows the Lord to determine the steps (Proverbs 16:9). More-over, as you begin to maintain balance, your schedule will feel more doable, and you will have more margin in your life.

Balance Is Not...A Life Free of Conflict and Difficulty

Consider the enormous difference between the peacekeeper and the peacemaker. The peacekeeper works tirelessly to avoid conflict and preserve the *appearance* that "all is well, no conflict here." The peacemaker is determined to have true inner peace, and will therefore live from the truth and deal openly and honestly with conflict. James 3:17-18 says, "The wisdom that comes from heaven is first of all pure. It is also peace loving, gentle at all times, and willing to yield to others. It is full of mercy and the fruit of good deeds. It shows no favoritism and is always sincere. And those who are peacemakers will plant seeds of peace and reap a harvest of righteousness."

A life of balance pursues a heart of peace. Though we bear God's image, and Jesus forgives us of our sin, we still sin, we're still selfish, and we still forget to love others the way Jesus has loved us. And since that's just true, there will be conflict. The question is, will you come through your relational breakdowns more pure, holy, and forgiving? Or will you harbor bitterness and poison your soul? A truly balanced woman will face conflict with dignity, security, humility, and love.

To keep balance and perspective in all seasons, we must dispel the idea that we're supposed to be "on" in every situation. Thank the Lord, He's much more merciful than that! And yet His provision is so abundant that He, being "on" all the time, will powerfully work through us even in our lowest of times. Balance is not summed up by the picture of what is happening on the outside. It is dictated by the truth transforming us on the inside. Thank You, Jesus.

Precious Lord,

You are all I need. You are my strength and my portion. Help me, Lord, not to look to the latest fad or fashion to determine my worth. May I never judge my value by what I produce. Help me instead to see from Your perspective. As I embrace Your values and make them my own, I will begin to change from the inside out. Give me a clearer picture of what balance looks like for me in this season I'm in. Help me not to compare and then despair. Help me, instead, to fix my eyes on You. I need You every hour. Amen.

Steps Toward Health

- If I am currently in a valley, I will resist the temptation to compare myself with those who are not. I will say, "Okay, I can't do _____, but I can do _____."
- If I am currently in a place of peace and plenty, I will resist the temptation to think that life is good because I am good. Life is good because God is good, and I will use my strength to help someone who needs a hand.
- If necessary, I will change my thinking in regard to what a "successful day" looks like. I will try to be open and flexible toward the changing needs of each new day.

Try This

- Write down the five things you value most in this world. Do your time investments reflect your values?
- Spend some extra time this week in prayer. Ask the Lord to give you a sense of what He is working on in you. Write it down, tuck it in your Bible, and continually pray about it until you see maturity in that area.
- Take a personal inventory of your motivations. Are you consistently doing or pursuing anything so others will think _____? Ask the Lord to help you step away from this pursuit, and allow that empty place to be filled by Him.
- Meditate this week on the fact that God loves you just for who you are and not for what you've accomplished. Allow yourself to be filled with joy at the thought. Once you've taken hold of this truth, don't let it get away from you.

Balance Application

To some degree, we're all products of our environment. And yet as Francis Frangipane, author and pastor, once said, "We must determine to allow nothing and no one to shape us, not even our personal experiences—unless they are consistent with the promises of God." To live within the promises of God, we must guard our hearts from the poisons of bitterness and jealousy. To maintain true balance, we must honestly assess our circumstance and then look for and find the place of greatest fruitfulness. This is how we gain ground even in the deepest valleys.

Study Time

1. Think about Ruth again. She was a widow in a foreign land who worked long hours under the sun to help provide for her mother-in-law and herself. Ruth did not have an easy life, but she truly was a woman of honor. Read Ruth 4:13-17.

2. Describe in your own words Ruth's struggles and the outcome.

3. How often do you notice God making something magnificent out of something menial? (Write down or discuss other times you've seen this happen in the Bible and in modern-day life.)

4. Where are you in your own process (for example, waiting, working, reaping)?

5. How is your attitude in relation to where you are right now? (If you're struggling, be honest about it. Ask for prayer and allow God to speak to your heart.)

6. To give a "sacrifice of praise" is to thank and worship God even when it is difficult to do. The sacrifice of praise puts feelings aside and hangs on to faith instead. Giving God the thanks He deserves will sometimes cost us something. Pause and thank Him by faith for His promise to meet *all* your needs. He is still faithful, and He will make something beautiful of your life if you let Him.

Personal Reflection

1. In what ways have you "compared and then despaired"? What does that person have that you so long for? Spend some time

with Jesus and ask Him for a more accurate picture of her life and yours. May you pray today with a fresh perspective!

2. When it comes to others' opinions and how you present to a watching world, what area of your life has too much of a hold on you (e.g., fashion, weight, finances, intellect, social acquaintances)? Write out a prayer of surrender. Put God in His rightful place in your life. May His opinion and perspective matter most of all. Our lives are meant to be a shining light in a dark world—and of course it matters how we present to a watching world—but most of us know the difference between a desire for others to know the love of Jesus and the desperate need for others to approve of us.

3. Consider your answer to the question above and—as an act of faith—loosen your grip on what has occupied too much space in your life. Offer it to Jesus and ask Him to show you what faith and freedom look like instead. Engage your faith, walk in holy confidence, and determine that Jesus alone is enough for you! This is an important step to freedom!

This Week's Goal:

_____

_____

_____

God's Promise to Me:

_____

_____

_____

What Keeps You Balanced, Grounded?

I seem to be able to recognize when I'm out of balance. I get alone with God as quick as I can with my Bible, my journal, my gratitude notebook, sometimes at the beach, or the library, or my dining room table, but I stay there until I hear from my Father and I feel the peace that passes all understanding. That's how I know I'm back in balance.

—Jane

Three

What Balance Is

*All of us must quickly carry out the tasks assigned
us by the one who sent me, for there is little time left
before the night falls and all work comes to an end.*
JOHN 9:4 TLB

When I think back to the times I was most out of balance both physically and spiritually, I shudder. That was when I was most depleted and distracted. More than 30 years ago I carried 35 extra pounds. My weight (and my stomach hanging over my jeans) was the first thing I thought about in the morning and the last thing I fretted about at night. Was I a fruitful Christian back then? I believe so, but I wasn't nearly as fruitful as I could have been because I was imprisoned and distracted by my own physical imbalance.

My mind also recalls a time when I was spiritually out of whack. I'd committed to too many things, and I am quite sure I did few of them well. I wince when I think of how I whipped out the door with my jacket hanging by one sleeve and my arms wrapped around my purse, my Bible, and my planner. My keys were in my mouth, and I yelled through pursed lips, "Dinner is in the oven!" I imagine my new neighbor walking by in fascination and wondering, *Wow, who's that gal? I want what she has!* Not!

Through painful circumstances beyond my control, as well as messes

I've made for myself, I have finally found a form of balance that works even when life doesn't. Through pressing into the Lord during times of testing, I learned a profound concept. I pray I can communicate it in a way you can quickly take hold of and apply.

Encarta Dictionary defines *balance* this way: "A state in which various elements form a satisfying and harmonious whole and *nothing is out of proportion or unduly emphasized at the expense of the rest*" (emphasis added).

Now that we have put away the notion that the balanced woman is one who keeps it together at all times, we can examine the true components of balance.

The True Components of Balance

Everyone's life involves these three components to some degree (I will interchange each of these three terms throughout the book):

1. Input (or Nourishment)

2. Output (or Response)

3. Rest (or Replenishment)

When we overemphasize either input or output at the expense of the other, we have imbalance. Let's look at these three components as the three levers in life. As long as you live, you will need to *receive* nourishment so you won't become malnourished. And to remain healthy, you'll need to *respond* to what's been deposited in you. And finally, you'll need consistent *rest* from your labors (both physically and spiritually) so your body, mind, and soul can heal. What will change through the varying seasons of life is the *degree* to which you do these things.

When I was sick in bed, I couldn't even consider training to run a race. I could, however, work on range of motion with my joints so I wouldn't get arthritis. Though my output (when compared to a healthy person) seemed like a dismal failure, for me it was how I maximized my potential. Applying myself to that small task took care of my joints—and now I can ride my road bike at a steady, fast pace and recover well afterward.

As I mentioned earlier, part of holding your ground (and gaining it) is honestly assessing your circumstance and then finding the greatest place of fruitfulness amid it all. In every situation, there is the best way to nourish yourself, the best way to respond to what's been deposited in you, and the best way to be replenished.

We wander away from balance when we neglect, forget, or think we don't need all three of these components in our lives. We can't eat a lot and never exercise, we can't exert ourselves constantly without food, and we cannot—must not—neglect our God-given times of rest.

> In every situation, there is the best way to nourish yourself, the best way to respond to what's been deposited in you, and the best way to be replenished.

As we come to understand the components of balance, we will also come to grasp the *fluidity* of balance. In other words, these components will adjust to our seasons and circumstances of life.

Throughout much of this book, we will look at our physical and spiritual nourishment (input), our physical and spiritual exercise (output), and our physical and spiritual replenishment (rest). I'll offer tangible tips to help you hold your ground on the bad days and gain new ground on the good days. At first glance, one would think a book on balance should address how we juggle all our roles in life. To me, this is like managing symptoms. If we take a deeper look at what we allow into our lives, and how we exert ourselves and react to life, and how we are replenished—if we manage our lives at *this* level—we will get to the core of where we put our time and why.

As we develop the mind-set that God has great nourishment for us physically and spiritually, we will become more alive in Christ. We will go through our days with a sense of expectation, knowing He has things He wants to deposit in us. We will pause and really taste the food He has provided for us (physical input), and we will marvel at the creative ways He speaks to us throughout the day (spiritual input). We will also come to understand our responsibility as His children to be open and ready to be used by Him wherever and whenever He says. We will exercise our physical bodies and bring them into a healthy balance, and we will stretch ourselves spiritually to affect the world around us (physical and spiritual output). Finally, we will understand the command and invitation to rest—a blessed gift from a Father who knows what we need (physical and spiritual replenishment).

When we live with the constant sense of the ebb and flow of nourishment, response, and replenishment, we will find balance wherever life takes us.

A Balanced Woman Is Someone Who...

- Runs around with her little ones outside for a while, even though she's cleaning the house to prepare for company.
- Refuses to allow the rat-race culture to dictate her pace.
- Consistently prioritizes time with her loved ones.
- Gives the benefit of the doubt, believes the best, and refuses (as a rule rather than the exception) to read between the lines or take things personally.
- Would rather bless than impress (wise words from my pastor's wife).
- Dares to say no to something she's not called to, even though she might disappoint others.
- Senses a call on her life and dares to say yes, even though she feels unqualified.
- Guards and protects her time with the Lord.
- Gives herself the gift of exercising several times a week.
- Is willing to interrupt her workout if a friend needs prayer or her child needs a hug.
- Pauses to acknowledge God's presence several times a day.
- Looks for God's purpose and counts on His provision even in crisis or valley.

- Refuses a busy, harried lifestyle.
- Gives herself (and her children) plenty of time to get out the door.
- Is willing to push herself beyond what's comfortable, for the purpose of growth.
- Is teachable.
- Is flexible.
- Has self-control.
- Hates gossip.
- Loves peace.
- Looks at difficult people with God in mind.
- Holds tight to faith, hope, and love.

Father God,

You have provided everything I need to live a life of fullness. Overwhelming victory is mine because of Your power mightily at work within me. May I live and move from that place of power rather than from a place of stress, insecurity, and defeat. Help me lay hold of all You have made available to me. I long to be balanced, unhurried, fruitful, and at peace. Bring me to that place of promise. In Your precious name I pray, amen.

Steps Toward Health

- In relation to the three levers in life—input, output, and rest—I will take an honest look at whether a lever has been unduly emphasized in my life.
- I will ask God to show me the most tangible way to maintain balance in this area.
- I will share this pursuit with a godly friend and ask for feedback.

- I will remember that it took a series of choices to lead me out of balance, and it will take a series of good choices to lead me back again.
- I will remind myself every single day that I am on the path to greater physical and spiritual health.

Try This

- Plan within the next couple of days to take a brisk 20- to 45-minute walk. Start making this a habit.
- Go to bed a little earlier tonight. If you have little ones, allow yourself to rest during their naps.
- This week, eat less and pray more. See what happens. (Important note: If you have the eating disorder anorexia, please disregard the invitation to eat less and follow your doctor's advice. Perhaps your challenge will be to eat more and pray more than you typically do. Also, spend some time waiting and listening to what the Lord might say to you today.)
- Say no when you know you should.
- At the end of each week, do a "balance inventory" and make note of what you did well and where you still need to grow.

Balance Application

With the demands of life pressing in on all sides, it is far too easy to lose touch with nourishment, response, and replenishment. And yet this is at the root of all we do and why. When we look closely at what we put into our bodies (and our souls), how (or if) we exercise our faith and our fitness, and to what extent we replenish ourselves, *we will see a clear picture of why we feel the way we do.* Once we learn and apply the basic components of a healthy, balanced life, we give ourselves the gifts of strength, perspective, and energy, with room to grow.

Study Time

1. In 1 Samuel 1 we read about Hannah, a woman deeply loved by her husband, Elkanah, but who was barren. Hannah was teased and tormented by Peninnah, Elkanah's other wife, who could have children. This broke Hannah's heart, and she cried out to God for mercy. Read 1 Samuel 1:19-27.

2. When Hannah's prayers were answered, what did she do?

3. Now read 1 Samuel 2:1-10.

4. As you read Hannah's prayer of praise, meditate on the sovereignty of God. What are at least four truths you can glean from this passage and apply to your own life?

5. When you think of God being fully in control, are you able to trust Him with what weighs you down and stresses you out? If not, why not?

6. Pray for an increased sense of His presence in your life.

Personal Reflection

1. Read once more through the list titled *A Balanced Woman Is…* Write down three statements that may not reflect where you are right now, but do speak of where you want to be someday. Write out a prayer asking God to grant you this desire of your heart (He *loves* to answer these kinds of prayers!).

2. Picture your life a year from now. What habits or tendencies do you want gone from your life, and what habits and/or mind-sets do you want firmly in place? Find a corresponding promise from Scripture and anchor yourself to God's Word. Pray this passage, rehearse this passage, and revisit this passage until you know it by heart.

3. How do you suppose God feels about you on your worst day? Scripture tells us nothing can *ever* separate us from God's love.

Write out a faith-declaration asserting God's commitment to you regardless of your ever-changing opinions about yourself. This will be great nourishment for your soul.

This Week's Goal:

_____

_____

_____

God's Promise to Me:

_____

_____

_____

What Keeps You Balanced, Grounded?

First thing in the morning, I do my devotions...before any social media. It grounds me and gets me moving in the right direction. When life and work get tough, I remember whom I'm working for and living for...Jesus!

—Khris

Four

You're Not in Over Your Head

Stand up and praise the LORD your God,
who is from everlasting to everlasting.
NEHEMIAH 9:5 NIV

I pulled my hood over my head as the winds blew and the gray clouds began to shift. I watched the ocean waves gather momentum just before crashing against the pier. This was not ideal weather for a day at the ocean, but my boys begged to try surfing just once before our vacation came to an end.

The strength and the force of the waves surprised me as I nervously watched my young sons fumble for balance on their surfboards. Thankfully, they stayed close to shore and were well within my reach should I need to get to them.

Another gust of wind swept my bookmark into the air. I chased it down and put it back in its place. Just as I glanced up again, I noticed panicked looks on both Jake's and Luke's faces. My heart rate sped up as I watched the undercurrent quickly sweep them farther from the shore. They paddled and paddled with their hands, but to no avail. The strength of the water pulled them far out of reach.

Just as I was getting ready to run to them, the lifeguard stood up and put a megaphone to his mouth. "You two boys on the boards, don't panic! Just stand up! Just stand up! The water is only four feet deep even way out there. You can do it. Stand up!"

Jake and Luke looked up at the lifeguard and decided to listen to him. Even though they were far from shore and felt captive to the strong current, they bravely hopped off their boards and found solid ground beneath their feet. They pressed through the current, and within moments they were safely ashore. It was as simple as that.

Choosing to Stand Up

Even though Jake and Luke *meant* to stay close to the beach, they were carried 30 yards from shore. The situation looked a little scary, and they *seemed* to be in over their heads, but they found their way back simply by standing up. That's what we're going to do today.

Imagine if I would have said to myself, *Oh well, my boys are too far out of reach now. I can't get to them. I will really miss them.* Of course, that is preposterous, and human life is far more valuable than any health goals we may have. And yet how often do we allow ourselves to give up and let go of something God wants us to have?

The enemy of our souls whispers words of defeat in our ears, and we are often quick to believe him. We've all heard familiar words like, "You'll never catch up now" or "Now you've blown it" or "Why can't you get it together?" or "You have no self-control!" Every one of these berating statements will diminish our souls. Furthermore, they're in direct conflict with the promises God has made to us. Even if we *have* messed up or struggle with self-control, God's promises are *for us*, today, right here, right now. It took me a long time to learn to reject such defeating thoughts, but as I filled my mind with the promises of God, my whole perspective changed.

> The enemy of our souls whispers words of defeat in our ears, and we are often quick to believe him.

It all starts with our perspective of where we are now and where we *could* be. Dear sister, wherever you are, God has more for you. Maybe you intended to keep your weight within a healthy range, but the currents of life have swept you to a place that feels out of control. Or maybe your weight is fine, but you know God is calling you to a healthier diet so you will feel better and live stronger. Perhaps you are in a spiritual rut and longing for fresh nourishment from God that will strengthen you spiritually. Well, you are in the right place!

Today we are going to declare that we are not as out of control as we may feel. The road back to health isn't unattainable; it just requires that we face the current that swirls about us, jump in right where we are, and determine to stand on what we know to be true. We can do this.

Nourishing Your Physical Body

It's always good for us to remember that food is a gift from God. Food is meant for the nourishment of our bodies, the repairing of cells for the promotion of health, energy storage, and *occasionally* for only enjoyment. Some of our fondest memories come from times of breaking bread and sharing meals with our loved ones. Unfortunately, we sometimes put too much emphasis on satisfying our taste buds. We try to numb our pain, drown out our frustrations, and use food as a default when we're stressed. We have thus lost the essence of the purpose of food. God is our Source and food is a gift. When we look to food as our source—a place we turn to when life gets to be too much for us—we fall out of balance.

Let's look at what food is not for.

Food is not for drowning our sorrows. "Surely he took up our pain and bore our suffering" (Isaiah 53:4 NIV). Jesus carries our sorrows. He will go to the source of our ache and bring healing and truth there if we ask Him to. He will bring freedom and clarity where we've known only pain and confusion. Our kids will at times break our hearts, friends sometimes betray us, and loved ones eventually pass away. But food in any of these instances will not serve as nourishment. In fact, it will *stand* in the way of the nourishment that comes from God. When you are overcome with sadness or sorrow, try praying and fasting instead.

Or sit in God's presence with a notebook and write down what He speaks to your heart.

Food is not an outlet for our anger. "Refrain from anger and turn from wrath; do not fret—it leads only to evil" (Psalm 37:8 NIV). Eating when you're angry only feeds your inability to practice self-restraint in difficult situations. I remember one day, years ago, when my boys were little and at each other all day long. The dog had a bladder infection, which caused obvious problems, and the neighbor boy purposely put a handful of gravel in our pool because he heard it would stop up the filter. On top of that, the city was flushing the fire hydrants, which caused my load of white clothes to be covered in rust spots. I was beside myself with anger and frustration.

Many times in the past, a day like that would prompt me to pull out a carton of ice cream and a spoon. But I was determined to overcome my unhealthy habits, and even more determined to find out what God's power could do in my real-life tough situations. I learned that eating when you're angry doesn't help the situation. Next time you're mad and find yourself reaching for food, get away from the kitchen, go for a brisk walk, and pray.

Food is not a cure for boredom. "Restore to me the joy of your salvation and grant me a willing spirit, to sustain me" (Psalm 51:12 NIV). The next time you're tempted to eat because you're bored, try calling someone who needs a word of encouragement, take the neighbor a bouquet of flowers, or do whatever else God puts on your heart.

Food is not meant only to fuel us. It is for enjoyment too. "Nehemiah said, 'Go and enjoy choice food and sweet drinks, and send some to those who have nothing prepared. This day is sacred to our Lord. Do not grieve, for the joy of the LORD is your strength'" (Nehemiah 8:10 NIV). Sometimes we're called to celebrate and enjoy food. These events provide us with great release, encouragement, and a reminder of the Lord's faithfulness. When we take a vacation, we plan for it, save for it, and look forward to it with great anticipation. Vacations are sweet because they are a departure from our normally busy lives. In the same way, we can "budget" and plan for party foods and desserts. As our healthy, balanced diet becomes a way of life, we will be able to fully enjoy and embrace times of celebration.

Father in heaven,

I'm thankful that nothing is too hard for You. Even if things seem out of control, they never are. I want to pursue a balanced life. Give me the courage to step through the waves of impulse and put my feet on solid ground. Increase my knowledge and understanding of what it means to live a healthy, holy life. I don't want to make my body an idol so that it becomes my obsession and focus. I want to make such good choices that I will no longer be distracted by my health. I want my health to serve me so I can better serve You. Help me to get there, Lord. In Your precious name, I pray, amen.

Steps Toward Health

- I will take an honest look at when and why I eat. If I consistently go toward food when what I really need is for God to refresh my soul and impart to my heart a fresh dose of wisdom and insight, I will pause and pray instead. I will humbly confess my need, and then I'll ask for the divine insight to discern the underlying issue whenever I'm driven to food instead of Jesus. I will ask the Lord for grace and power to choose wisely from now on.

- If my eating habits are balanced and disciplined, I will give thanks and pray for a friend who struggles with food.

- If I struggle with an eating disorder, with manipulating my food, or with using portion control to control my life, I will commit to seeking out a mentor/counselor/friend with whom I can be honest so I can intentionally pursue healing and freedom in this area.

- I will put my foot down on the promises of God, do His will, and know I will be safe. (Pick a promise from the Bible and stand on it. Need a verse? Try this one: "I can do everything God asks me to with the help of Christ who gives me the strength and power" (Philippians 4:13 TLB).)

Try This

- When you notice the stress level picking up in your day, get away from the kitchen or the candy aisle and find a place to pray. You will truly be refreshed.

- Take a moment each morning to commit your day to the Lord. Ask Him for added grace to change your eating habits. Ask for a heightened sensitivity to His Spirit so you'll notice when you're about to grab food without thinking.

- Practice self-restraint in other areas of your life, for example, with phone calls, gossip, TV, reading junk, shopping, computer games, Internet surfing, or emailing. Self-restraint takes practice, but I know you can do it.

Balance Application

As we continue to grow in the Lord, we will find ourselves turning to Him for our soul's deepest needs. The book of Jeremiah says the heavens shrink back in horror when they see us drinking from "muddy puddles" when Jesus is the wellspring of life (my own paraphrase). I try to imagine the cloud of witnesses shrinking back in shock every time I look to something other than God to medicate my pain. The heavens can't imagine why we wouldn't draw from the Source that is free and perfect. If our lives have been out of balance with too much dietary input, may we bend our knee before the Lord and recommit ourselves to finding our fullness in Him.

Study Time

1. More important than the food we do or do not eat is a heart set on obeying God. Read Daniel 1:8-20.

2. Why would it have seemed natural for Daniel to indulge in food that was not God's best for him?

3. Again, occasionally, party foods are great—but how often do you allow yourself indulgences that are less than God's best for you simply because of your surroundings?

4. Something happens spiritually when we set our hearts on doing God's will—when we say no to ourselves so we can say yes to God. Look again at the passage in Daniel. Describe some of Daniel's God-given gifts.

5. How did Daniel's gifts affect the spiritual climate around him?

6. Much of what comforts the flesh weakens the soul. Can an excess indulgence in your life be replaced with a more earnest pursuit of God's purpose and power? Imagine how this would affect the world around you.

7. Pray for more of Him and less of you.

Personal Reflection

1. How would you describe your relationship with food? In what circumstances do you most often default to food (e.g., stress, fun, social gatherings, anger, fear, boredom)? What would a healthier approach look like for you? Write out a prayer and ask God for wisdom and direction for your next steps.

2. To what degree do you involve Jesus when it comes to your physical health? Do you pray about your choices? Do you ask Him to guide and guard your efforts? How might you more intentionally involve Him in your health journey?

3. We all tend to have a default diet, repeatedly eating the same foods. If this applies to you, consider how you might bring balance to your diet with a new food. God is always up to something new, and He cares about you! What new food item might be good for you?

This Week's Goal:

_____

_____

_____

God's Promise to Me:

_____

_____

_____

What Keeps You Balanced, Grounded?

Practically speaking, I can handle stress and busy so much better when I leave room in my schedule to keep my house in order. I leave myself time to clean, do laundry, and grocery shop.

—*Kristen*

Five

Be Nourished

Feast there in the Presence of GOD, your God.
Celebrate everything that you and your families have
accomplished under the blessing of GOD, your God.
DEUTERONOMY 12:7 MSG

When was the last time you truly enjoyed a meal? I don't mean the last time you ate food that simply tasted good. When was the last time you sat down before a meal—setting aside every other thing vying for your attention—and *pondered* all the aspects of that meal: the taste, the time, and the provision? There is something powerful about pausing before a meal long enough to feel overwhelmed by the goodness of God. Isn't it something that you not only *get* to eat a warm meal, but you also have a choice in what foods to eat? While millions are starving, you have been provided for. What would happen if we acquired a *new* habit of thanksgiving—a consistent, sincere, heartfelt expression of thanks to God for His goodness to us—before we even took our first bite of food?

Think of how you feel about food after you've recovered from the flu. That first bite of real food tastes like a treasure. Back when I was very sick and every area of my life seemed to be falling apart, I wrote this in my journal: *Thank You, Lord, for taking away. For when we have again, we know to be thankful.*

Scientific studies have proven time and time again that a thankful heart is good for our health. This is wonderful, but even more importantly, a thankful heart reminds us to acknowledge God's presence and provision in everything we do. Food tastes so much better when we pause for a moment, pray for those who have less than we do, thank the Lord for His provision, and then acknowledge that blessing by truly *tasting* each bite that nourishes us.

When we invite Jesus into our lives and ask Him to bring health and wholeness to the very depths of our being, He will do far beyond all we could ask or think (Ephesians 3:20 NKJV). We are not destined for struggle or to just get by. No, "overwhelming victory" belongs to us because we belong to Him (Romans 8:37).

> When we invite Jesus into our lives and ask Him to bring health and wholeness to the very depths of our being, He will do far beyond all we could ask or think.

Do not look down at your inability—look up at Him. We need to raise our expectation of what God will do for us even in this area of nourishing ourselves. God's promises are rich and true for every area of our lives. C.S. Lewis wrote,

> Indeed, if we consider the unblushing promises of reward and the staggering nature of the rewards promised in the Gospels, it would seem that Our Lord finds our desires, not too strong, but too weak. We are half-hearted creatures, fooling about with drink and sex and ambition when infinite joy is offered us, like an ignorant child who wants to go on making mud pies in a slum because he cannot imagine what is meant by the offer of a holiday at the sea. We are far too easily pleased.[1]

We intentionally eat right and manage our portions so we'll be nourished and strengthened to live healthy, fruitful lives. Of course, it's okay to enjoy the occasional treat; it's good for the soul to celebrate around the table! It's even okay to have popcorn for dinner once in a while. But as a rule, food must not master us. It must not control, defeat, or distract us. God has a high calling on our lives, and we cannot afford to be distracted and addicted to the things of this world. If we center our lives on food, we can't center our lives on God. What goes in us will eventually catch up with us—so we need to be careful about what we feed ourselves. Let's look at some tangible tips for healthy eating.

Food Laws to Live By

Stay away from fad diets. Begin to think more about a lifestyle change. We live in such a quick-fix society that we have come to refuse anything less than a quick solution. But quick solutions quickly fade. Anything worth having takes time to acquire, and discipline with food is definitely worth having. The goal is to have your input balance your output. Change your thinking to this: *I am going to take control of what I put in my mouth. I will not be at the mercy of the moment. God has made a way for me.*

Give up soda (or at least cut back). Soda is a hot button, and you will have to decide for yourself about this one. I used to drink diet soda every day, but when I was so sick I wanted to die, I learned a few things about what it means to "treat myself." Every time I "treated myself" to soda, I drained my bone strength, made it difficult for my body to absorb certain nutrients, deprived myself of water, and lost my taste for water and juice. Plus, it's hard to lose weight while still getting proper nourishment if soda is part of your diet. I gave myself a fighting chance when I changed my mind about the impact my "treats" were having on me. You decide on this one. Even less is better.

Drink plenty of water. Water does wonders for us. From aiding in metabolism to lubricating our joints, from transporting wastes to regulating our body temperature, water works *for* us in the way soda works against us. Often women will retain water when they don't drink enough water. I encouraged my husband to start with this one discipline in his pursuit toward health, and in five weeks he had lost ten pounds.

Budget treats. If I eat a candy bar in a dark closet, is it still fattening? I used to do mental gymnastics to justify my choices. We touched on budgeting treats earlier, but just a reminder—when you plan for treats, you can eat them out in the open without shame or guilt. And they taste so much better that way.

Keep it colorful. Don't overload on any one food item. Carrots are a great food, but if you eat too many of them, you'll turn orange. Make sure you eat a nice balance of fruits, vegetables, grains, and proteins. Varying opinions weigh in on how one should combine these foods. Listen to your body (and your intestines). You'll know if something agrees with you or not. Keep your portions small, and never eat to the point of feeling stuffed.

Minimize artificial sweetener intake. This obviously doesn't apply to diabetics or others with health issues. It is also important to note that this is just my opinion. You talk it over with your doctor and decide. If you are basically healthy, I encourage you to keep your artificial sweetener intake to a minimum. We still don't know all the effects these sweeteners will have on our long-term health. Also, ingesting too many foods with artificial sweetener creates the illusion that you can eat more than you should. It's better to get used to smaller portions and healthier food choices.

Remember the metabolic rule. If you go longer than about three hours without eating, your metabolism will start to drop. Your body thinks it's going into famine and therefore provides for itself by slowing down the rate you burn calories. This will keep you alive if you're stranded in the wilderness, but if you're not truly in a famine, you'll gain weight because you won't be as quick to burn up calories. It's best to eat a small protein snack between meals (nuts, nutritional bar, yogurt, protein shake, apples and peanut butter, and so on). This will keep your metabolism where you want it. Also, you won't be as hungry when you get to your next mealtime, which will help to keep you from eating more than you need.

Choose vitamins and supplements wisely. It's important to educate yourself on vitamins and herbs because not all of them are right for you. Just as each of us is different from the other, our strengths and deficiencies vary. Some herbs will help one person and make another sick. Some herbs are harmful if mixed with other herbs, and certain vitamins can be toxic when taken in large doses. Supplementing your diet is great because you're probably not getting all the nourishment you need from food, but it is equally important to do your homework and find the supplements that are right for you.

Don't eat at night. Again, make this a rule rather than the exception. Determine not to eat after 8:00 p.m. and stick to it. Once you get used to it, I guarantee you will sleep better, feel better in the morning, and more easily manage your weight. If you want, give yourself a break on the weekends. One caveat here: Those who consistently wake up in the middle of the night for about a two-hour period (e.g., from 2:00–4:00, or 3:00–5:00) may do so because their blood sugar drops in the middle of the night. If that's you, you may benefit from eating a small, healthy snack just prior to bedtime.

Practice partial fasts. This idea seems to conflict with the metabolic rule, but let me explain. More important than our metabolism is a heart not bound by habit, addiction, or selfishness. If we dance around, make provision for, and demand that we have certain areas in our lives, it's good to look at those areas. When we lay those things at the altar for the purpose of having more of Christ's influence in our lives, something powerful happens.

I even put this into practice with my kids when they were young. When I noticed a certain video game, toy, or TV show becoming so important to them that they were ugly if they didn't get it, I showed them they indeed *could* live without their treasured item. After a few days I could see relief on the faces of my boys, as though they had conquered something themselves. During their teenage years, they were quick to notice whenever something became more important to them than their relationship with Christ. You can fast from food,[2] from your phone, from TV, from sweets, or simply from talking too much. Every time you lift something up to the Lord and say, "Lord, here. Please take this so I can have more of You," you'll will find yourself more blessed and free (I always ask God to take care of my metabolism during my partial fasts—and He always does). If you're pregnant, nursing, diabetic, or have certain medical problems, fast from something other than food.

Use your strength. When you feel strong, use that strength to make the best choices in your diet. When you feel weak, don't absolve yourself from making good choices. Just pray, do your best, and hang on until the storm has passed. When I was on a never-ending diet cycle years ago, I would blow it on a Wednesday and say, "Oh, well. I'll start again on Monday," giving myself four more days to eat too much. When you really think about it, we blow it for a *moment*. We don't need to count the whole day a loss. If we acknowledge it as a moment, we can adjust our "output" by getting a little more exercise and really not lose any ground. Still, try to resist the temptation of continually relying on exercise to make up for overindulging. The tendency to overeat must be conquered, and it can be.

Deal with your idols. Maybe you have a healthy relationship with food, but many don't. If you overindulge when unpleasant emotions surface, don't berate yourself, and don't numb-out on food. Instead, rejoice that you have somewhere to go with your heartbreak. Jesus knows all about your battles and your bruises. And He really wants to heal you and strengthen you. So during those crisis moments, turn your back on food and turn your face toward Jesus. Invite Him into the center of your struggle and see what He'll do. Determine to crush your idol every time you're tempted to polish it and give it a central place in your life.

But maybe your idol isn't one of overindulgence, but one of control and starvation, depression and obsession with body image. If that's you, I pray you have a trusted counselor to walk alongside you, and that you'll be brutally honest about what drives you so you can come to a place where you trust Jesus to lead you. Just remember, an idol is like a parasite—it drains the life and strength right out of you. Catering to your need for control and perfection through food will only ensure weakness, sickness, and certain captivity. Jesus wants you to live full and free, healthy and strong, and you can trust Him to help you find a healthier path.

Life Laws to Be Strengthened By

Use your strength. Apply this law in life as well. On the days you feel good, make an extra meal, clean out a closet, or do an involved craft with your kids. On your weaker days, you'll be glad you did.

Garbage in, garbage out. This is an age-old law, one that has proven true over and over again. Whatever we expose ourselves to will eventually bear fruit in our lives (be it good or rotten). It's prideful to think we can watch filthy movies, listen to lewd lyrics, or engage in low conversations without being affected by them. This charge is not to promote legalism—quite the opposite. This is a challenge to look around our lives and do some housecleaning for the expressed purpose of pursuing greater health and holiness. There's a significant difference between a prideful posture that boasts, "I would *never* watch such a thing!" and the heart that humbly says, "I just can't watch that. I care about my mind-set, my soul, and my health. Jesus wouldn't want me to be a part of that."

Less is more. You've heard this before, but it's worth repeating: Simplify your life. When we're spread too thin, our stress level goes up, we begin to take shortcuts in various areas of our lives, and our quality of life goes down. And we lose sight of the simple peace and joy Jesus so lovingly offers. When we commit to more than Jesus asks of us, we are at greater risk of falling into temptation, losing perspective of what is important, and of missing the spontaneous voice of God.

Often we become too busy because we have a hard time saying no, we want to impress somebody, we want something God hasn't provided yet, or we simply lack the faith to cut the extras from our lives.

Women often struggle with discontentment; this is one of the devil's greatest weapons. Think of Eve in the garden of Eden. She lived in a perfect place, and yet the devil convinced her she was *entitled to more.* When we think we're entitled to more than God is giving us now, we tend to grab stuff for ourselves, and our lives become cluttered and out of balance as a result. But when we become more focused, less stressed, and more reliant on God, something wonderful happens: We end up having *more.* More energy, more joy, more grace for others, and a better perspective.

One of my favorite verses is 1 Timothy 6:6: "Godliness with contentment is great gain" (NIV). Think about it. When we pursue a closer walk with God and respond to His upward call *while* embracing a heart of contentment for *where we are right now,* we gain. We have much to gain by doing less, doing it better, and waiting on God's timing for our lives.

Say no to yourself on a regular basis. "I strike a blow to my body and make it my slave so that after I have preached to others, I myself will not be disqualified for the prize" (1 Corinthians 9:27 NIV). Just because you can afford to buy something, eat something, or do something doesn't mean you should. Every day, in some small way, say no to yourself. Don't give yourself everything your heart desires; say no and make yourself deal with it. The Bible tells us to *exercise* self-control. That means we must put it into practice. Self-restraint is not a popular idea in this self-entitled world, and yet it's a precious fruit of the Holy Spirit—one that will keep us out of trouble if we stay close to the Lord and apply His principles to our lives.

Understand that continual self-indulgence leads to a drop in standard. "To learn, you must love discipline" (Proverbs 12:1). While we need to treat ourselves occasionally, to do so all the time would allow our indulgences to push us backward. No one is meant to live in "party mode," and the one who pursues such a lifestyle will quickly come to ruin. Take an honest inventory, search your heart, and see if you have become a slave to any indulgences or ones to which you make regular accommodation. Little treats here and there bless our days and give us a lift. But I'm not talking about those; I'm talking about the indulgences that have a hold on us. Indulgences we make provision for, ones that make us cranky if life gets in the way of our getting them.

Again, please understand. This inventory is not to promote legalism. It's for you to tighten up in your life so your time and energy are invested in moving forward into what God has for you. Ask the Lord to show you if an area in your life needs to be liberated by His power. He will deliver you if you allow Him to.

Take a vision inventory. Once or twice a year, get alone with God to wait, listen, and receive a fresh vision from Him. Ask the Lord to give you a glimpse of your next place of promise. Open your hands and ask Him what has to go so you can make room for what He has for you. Ask Him what obedience looks like in this season so you will be rightly positioned for the season to come. Ask Him what faith seeds need to go in the ground now so you can be ready for a future harvest later.

For example, maybe He'll call you to give a financial gift to a ministry that's doing great kingdom work. When you give God access to your finances, it tethers you even more to His vision on the earth today. *Where your treasure is, your heart is* (Matthew 6:21; Luke 12:34). And your gift supports another ministry, which reminds you we're all in this together. Maybe sowing a "future seed" is about signing up for classes or attending a conference that equips you for your next season. Or maybe that future seed is all about planting new seeds of God's Word into the soil of your heart—memorizing Scripture that will sturdy you for the road ahead. Whatever He asks of you, be quick to obey Him. Write down what He shows you and tuck it in your Bible. Keep it before you so you'll remember it when storms hit.

Take a moment now and consider the nourishment you receive through food and other things you are exposed to. Are your choices weakening you or strengthening you? Could you begin to take steps toward better health and wholeness even today? Initially it will take extra effort, but in the long run, you will be strengthened by the momentum of your healthy choices, and that strength will carry you. And remember, His mercies are new every morning and His faithfulness is great (Lamentations 3:23).

God in heaven,

You are all I need. Forgive me for the countless times I've looked to the things of this world to satisfy my hunger. Please, Lord, increase my hunger for You. Heighten my sensitivity to Your Spirit so I can sense ahead of time when I am about to choose less than Your best for me. I want my whole life to be nourished by You so I can be constantly aware of Your presence. Lord Jesus, I want more of You in me. Amen.

Steps Toward Health

- If my eating is completely out of control, I will repent of the imbalance I have allowed in my life. I will be thankful for Christ's forgiveness and His promise to help me.

- If I use food to control my life because of my obsession with body image, I will seek out a trusted counselor and be honest about my need for freedom. I refuse to be held captive by a lie. Freedom isn't found in a perfect body, but in a perfect Savior. I refuse to let my drive for perfection keep me from the truth of the freedom Jesus purchased for me.

- If I don't eat too much, but I eat all the wrong things, I will acknowledge that my body is the temple of the Lord. I will ask God's forgiveness for becoming lazy in my diet. I will seek His help as I make necessary adjustments.

- If I naturally eat well, I will thank the Lord for motivating me to do so. I will pray for the friend who struggles in this area. I will stay humble and not think for a moment that I am exceptional because I eat well. I will remember that pride goes before a fall. God has allowed me to gain victory over this area, and I will in turn intercede for someone else's victory.

Try This

- Don't weigh yourself more than once every two weeks. Put your focus on your health, and eventually your weight will fall into place.

- Don't allow yourself to eat sweets during the week. Treat yourself on the weekends.

- Make yourself eat something for breakfast that includes some protein (eggs, protein shake, peanut butter on an apple, and so on). You'll feel better and be less apt to crash and burn later in the day.

- Buy a cool water bottle and keep yourself hydrated throughout the day.

- If you must eat at a fast-food restaurant, choose a salad or grilled meat without the bun. Better yet, stop at a grocery store and pick up a bagged salad or go through their salad bar if they have one. Choose plenty of dark greens and vegetables.

- Walk away from toxic conversations, movies, and music.

- Tell yourself daily, "I am fearfully and wonderfully made. I am getting stronger and healthier every day!"

Balance Application

As I mentioned earlier, if you are in a good place, use your strength to gain extra ground. Make especially good choices and stick with them. If you are faltering and feeling weak, pray and ask for God's help. Don't give up completely. Just do your best and hold your ground. If you are in crisis mode, you may have no choice but to go without meals or to eat at irregular times. This is not the time to worry about your diet. Entrust yourself to your heavenly Father, and your life will adjust accordingly.

If you have an addictive background and/or unresolved issues of anger or unforgiveness, this chapter may do little more than get under your skin. The suggestions about not eating for the wrong reasons may cause you to feel defensive and angry. The most important thing for you right now is to get to the bottom of your feelings. The advice in this chapter is not meant to be a substitute for professional counsel, but rather a supplement to it. If this applies to you, I ask you, sister, to please go after wholeness and health. Let nothing deter you. Freedom is waiting for you.

Determine not to be overwhelmed by the amount of information in this chapter. You may need to read it a few times. Incorporate *one or two* of these principles at a time and make them a part of your everyday life. Come back to this chapter occasionally, and take inventory. When you're ready, add another discipline. Remember, God's grace is all yours. He is with you and will give you grace to abound in every good work! (2 Corinthians 9:8).

Study Time

1. Read 2 Samuel 11 and consider how temptation first presents itself. First David decided on his own to opt out of his God-given duty, which then positioned him to be tempted and distracted and eventually disgraced. Though overeating doesn't compare with adultery and murder, all these excesses originate from the same place—from a heart that wants its own way, not God's way. Think about the last time you overindulged (eating, drinking, spending, watching, and so on). What was that reason? How did you feel afterward?

2. Describe the thoughts that went through your head afterward.

3. Did those thoughts weaken you or strengthen you?

4. Describe at least four ways this incident affected your mental, physical, and spiritual health.

5. Spend some time praying through Psalm 23, and then reflect again on how wisely and faithfully the Savior leads us. We miss Him when we run ahead in angst or fall behind in apathy. May we stay in step with Him.

6. Read Romans 5:1-5. What makes us right in God's sight? What allows us to stand in that highest place of privilege? Describe what those terms mean to you.

7. What are the by-products of our faith?

8. Read verses 3-5 again. Why does God allow us to struggle?

9. Read and meditate on this beautiful passage one more time, slowly. Ask the Holy Spirit to fill your heart with God's love today.

Personal Reflection

1. This week we're looking at not only our input (how and why we nourish ourselves), but also how we personally respond to those choices. What have you noticed about the ripple effect of your most consistent choices to nourish yourself? What happens to your energy level, your self-talk, and your thought process? Write down your thoughts.

2. How much time do you spend berating yourself for falling short or for your "not enoughness"? How about if you decide today to be a little kinder to your soul? Write out a prayer asking God to help you love yourself and see yourself the way He loves you and sees you.

3. Change is difficult. Our flesh dies hard. Ask God to give you a fresh vision of the kind of health that's possible for you.

This Week's Goal:

_____

_____

_____

God's Promise to Me:

_____

_____

_____

What Keeps You Balanced, Grounded?

I travel. Even if it's to the backyard to look at God's majestic cre-ation. The wonder of wandering into His scenic splendor makes my heart connect with Him and makes everything reset and right again. I see His incredible love in all that surrounds us.

—*Christine*

Six

Get Your Body to Work as It Should

I discipline my body like an athlete, training it to do what it should. Otherwise, I fear that after preaching to others I myself might be disqualified.

1 Corinthians 9:27

I settled back, buckled my seat belt, and pulled out my notebook. I had a three-hour flight and was thankful for the extra time to study. At the time I was a fitness trainer, and my notes were opened to anatomy and physiology. I was lost in the material until I sensed the man sitting next to me peering over my shoulder. I looked over at him, smiled, and asked, "How are you doing today?"

He smiled back and said, "Fitness, huh?"

"Yes, sir," I replied.

Right away he told me his story. "One day my wife was doing the dishes and something outside caught her attention. She looked out the window, then at me, and said, 'Wow. That Bob is really in good shape.' I looked out the window to see our muscle-bound neighbor running by." My seatmate became more animated as he continued. "So I puffed up my chest, pulled in my gut, looked at my wife, and said, 'I can do that,' and within minutes, decked out in my workout clothes, I went outside for a run. I ran seven miles."

"What happened?"

His shoulders dropped as he sighed. "I damaged my Achilles ten-dons, and now I can barely walk straight. So what'd I do wrong?"

I could tell this guy could take some teasing, so I said, "You let your ego get the best of you!"

He sat back in his seat and said, "I know. I really blew it. I used to be in great shape, and I compared the guy I used to be to my bodybuilder neighbor. Now I can't run at all."

I encouraged him to remember the more important things in life, like loving his wife and being defined by who he is and not by what he produces. We had a great talk, and afterward he seemed to feel better.

I share this story because it's a perfect example of what happens to people every single day. We cannot compare ourselves to who we were years ago, nor can we compare ourselves to others. Backward and side-ways comparisons never produce good fruit. Negatively comparing our bodies now to how they used to be when we were younger yields no good fruit. Negatively comparing our bodies to those around us tends to produce despair, which drains the life energy right out of our souls. But to take inventory of where we are, how we got here, and where we sense God wants to take us, well, that's downright wise and takes great courage. So that's what we're going to do.

> Negatively comparing our bodies to those around us tends to produce despair, which drains the life energy right out of our souls.

Little Steps in the Right Direction

The only way to gain ground in physical fitness is to honestly assess:

- Where am I right now?

- What are my limitations?

- Are any circumstances or people consistently weakening my

resolve to move forward in faith and health? What would God have me do in these situations?

- Where would I like to be?
- How do I get there?

Once we honestly answer these questions, we're pointed in the right direction and ready to start. I cannot tell you how many times I was in excellent shape only to get injured, have a crisis, or be put on bed rest during pregnancy. Each time I reentered the ring, I was practically starting over. My first few trips back to the health club were so defeating because I knew in my head how to take fitness to the next level, and yet my body was weak and needed to be treated like a beginner. Once I got ahold of that fact, I decided to embrace the challenge as an opportunity to grow in humility, patience, focus, and discipline. I wrapped my arms around the struggle and gave myself permission to take one step at a time toward getting fit again.

The human body is so divinely wired that you can get it to do almost anything—as long as you ask it nicely. In other words, you—yes, you—are capable of doing the splits, running in a race, or doing push-ups (unless you've got a disability, although thousands with disabilities find ways around their disability to achieve a greater level of health). To get your body to do what seems beyond you, you must introduce the idea by taking little steps in that direction. Before we take another step in this direction, though, I'd like you to get a full physical. Tell your doctor of your plans to start a new exercise regimen and ask for his or her input based on the results of your examination.

Remember to work out within the boundaries of your personal health and limitations. One-size-fits all does not apply to exercise. Be wise about this, and be willing to start with baby steps. For instance, if you're dealing with adrenal fatigue, it's detrimental to your health to go all out with heavy sprints, drills, and extreme cardio. It's much better for you to back off the intensity and focus on moderation and consistency (and being consistent goes for your bedtime too—more on this later). If you have arthritic issues, you want to work on strengthening and lengthening your muscles—in other words, strength work and flexibility will help support your joints and alleviate some of your pain (but remember, cardio is good for you too). If you have asthma, you'll need a longer warm-up to give your body and your breathing time to prepare for the workout.

Berating yourself for your limitations will only push you backward. We all have our limitations, things that ail and inhibit us. You're not alone. But even with your limitations, you don't need to stay where you are right now. You can have a forward-moving plan that respects your limits but doesn't accept them as an excuse to stay stuck. No matter what your issue, never underestimate the power of small, consistent steps.

Over time, your body will not only respond to your requests, but it will help you get to where you're going. For instance, your goal may be to increase your flexibility—an excellent idea for anybody. Research strongly recommends a dynamic warm-up with movement before working out (a brisk walk on the treadmill or the first few minutes of a group fitness class). Then follow your cardio/strength workout with static stretching and deep, cleansing breaths. During the stretch portion of your workout, do not bounce or push yourself too far. Again, respect your limits and then work from there. If you keep this up and each day stretch a *little* further than the day before, eventually your body learns it's okay to stretch that far and adapts to what you're asking it to do. Before you know it, you've significantly increased your range of motion and eliminated many of your aches and pains. Isn't that amazing?

It's the same with running. As you gradually introduce your body to the idea of this kind of exertion, your body will read the consistent messages you're sending and eventually "help you out" by being more efficient with oxygen supply, heart/lung support, and recovery. Running is not for everybody, but every person is wired and made for some form of cardio exercise. Believe it or not, eventually your cardio exercise will grow easier and you will begin to feel better than you ever have before. The key is to take small steps, give consistent messages, and be patient with yourself. For our spiritual lives the Bible tells us to run with patient endurance (Hebrews 12:1). *Running with patience* sounds like an oxymoron, and yet the patient runner finishes strong. Proverbs 4:12 says, "If you live that kind of life, you'll not limp or stumble as you run" (TLB). Exercise wisdom as you gradually introduce your body to this kind of exercise, and you will go far.

An old adage in fitness says, "Take more ground on the good days." You know those days when you wake up and, for some reason, you just feel great? You have energy and focus, and you feel motivated. It's tempting to retrace your steps and ask, "Okay, what did I do right yesterday? What did I eat? How much sleep did I get?" and so on. Well, many trainers will tell you to go the extra mile on those days. Run farther, lift more, push harder. Take advantage of the strong days and gain more ground. This will compensate for those days when you do less.

I'm going to incorporate this theme throughout the rest of the book in dealing with both our physical and our spiritual health. One of our goals is to understand and embrace when it is healthy to push harder than we are used to and when it is wise to pull back and rest. *At the heart of true, lasting balance is the ability to read your health and your circumstances, and then adjust accordingly.* As you gear up to take your fitness to the next level, here are a few tips to keep in mind.

Tangible Tips as You Prepare for Exercise

Take an honest assessment. Assess where you are in your health and in your stage of life. Set realistic goals and make a plan that works for you. Do you work out better alone or with someone? Is it easier on your family if you exercise in the morning or at night? Know that God has created you to move, and He will honor your desire for a healthy body as long as you keep that desire balanced with other priorities.

Ask nicely. Be content to start where you need to. Resist the temptation to look around at where anyone else is in pursuit of health and fitness. Walk, lift, or stretch just beyond what is comfortable for you (more on this later).

Leave your comfort zone. To grow, we must continually push beyond what is comfortable. Once you have assessed your ability, continually ask your body to do a *little bit* more. As you push just beyond what is "normal" for you, you'll notice that your threshold increases, and you'll begin to gain ground in the area you're working. Ronald E. Osborn wrote, "Undertake something that is difficult; it will do you good. Unless you try to do something beyond what you have already mastered, you will never grow."

Don't give up what you've gained. It is much harder to get something back than it is to maintain it. Think about relationships, good habits, and skills. In every area of life, some aspects require our attention or we'll eventually lose them. Exerting a little bit of effort now is far easier than dealing with the consequences later. Keep that piece of wisdom in your mind when looking at exercise (and at life). Truly, you only need to exercise about three to four hours per week to enjoy great health. Some will work out more, others less; but four hours out of 168 is a small investment for the great returns you'll enjoy.

Understand atrophy. Let me further clarify the previous point. When we allow our good habits to get away from us, breakdown happens. Atrophy basically means breaking down or wasting away. Our muscles atrophy when we stop exercising either by choice or by illness or injury. Because of this, extensive time in bed after an injury, surgery, or illness is no longer advised. Doctors, nurses, and therapists encourage patients to get up and start moving so the healing process can continue and so their muscles won't waste away. If you experience a setback in exercise, it may seem that your gains come slower than your losses. But even so, press on.

Take more ground on the good days. I mentioned this already, but it must be at the forefront of your mind to continue forward movement. Try it. On your good days, push a little harder; you'll feel exhilarated by the challenge. You will also get a glimpse of your potential.

It takes energy to make energy. Just as it takes money to make money, it takes energy to make energy. Often people will tell me they don't exercise because they don't have the energy. With the exception of some underlying disease, exercise is the remedy for low energy. For several years after my battle with a disease, I struggled with fatigue. I was also an aerobics instructor at the time. I cannot tell you how many nights I was scheduled to teach and yet felt overwhelmed with exhaustion. I knew I had to show up to teach my class, so I pulled myself up by my bootstraps and got myself to the club.

I can honestly say that for every single time I taught a class despite sheer exhaustion, 95 percent of the time I left feeling great. It was only when I was on the verge of a cold or flu that the exercise made me even more tired. If you're dealing with just a slight cold, a light workout, lots of water, and a few minutes in the sauna might do wonders for you. But if you have a fever or the flu, do not exercise. It's time for bed, rest, and fluids as you can tolerate them.

But for the rest of you who battle fatigue only because of life responsibilities, I encourage you to exercise. Just try it. Invest a little energy on those tired days and see if you don't get positive results. It's important to note that when you first start exercising, you will feel more fatigued after exercise until you get used to it. In fact, one way to measure your progress in your overall health and fitness is to pay attention to how quickly you recover from your workouts. When you start to notice that you bounce back quicker and quicker, be encouraged. You're getting stronger!

Listen to your body. This may seem in conflict with my previous point, but read on. Another reason we should take small steps at a time is so we can pay attention to how our bodies are responding. Some days we will respond beautifully, and other days we will feel a bit rough afterward. One day at the end of an aerobics class, we took our recovery heart rate. I noticed one of my regular attendees had a perplexed look on her face. I asked her if she was okay. She replied, "I feel fine. I felt great during class, and yet I'm not recovering as efficiently as I usually do." I encouraged her to walk around a bit more, drink water, stay out of the sauna, and pay attention to how she was feeling. She wasn't in class the following week, and she told me later that she got the stomach flu that evening. She didn't feel it coming, but already her body was responding differently to exercise. The point is that once you get into a groove and are used to your workout program, it's easy to go on autopilot and not pay attention to how your body is responding. If you're sweating more than usual, if your heart rate goes up too fast, or you just don't feel the same, back off a bit, drink your water, and listen to your body.

Don't go through the motions. I used to teach an advanced-level step class. I was always intrigued by the various levels of workouts taking place in the same studio with the same choreography under the leadership of the same instructor. Some of my members were soaked in sweat, breathing hard, using full range of motion, and yipping and hollering when the effort got intense. Others stayed very close to their step, hardly moved their limbs, and were barely sweating and breathing. I always told my members to listen to their bodies and work at their own pace. I love it when people feel secure enough to take care of themselves during their workouts. But I have also seen others get frustrated with their lack of progress, even though they barely put anything into their exercise.

When you understand body mechanics, you will be able to get an intense workout doing the most basic of moves. For now, just remember to be fully present when exercising. Throw yourself into what you're doing. For instance, if you're walking, swing your arms. Make every move count and pay attention to your body when it hurts. Another reason not to just go through the motions is so we don't overlook this very important fact: If we are healthy enough to exercise, we are blessed indeed. May we never take that for granted. Just as food tastes much better when we're fully present and fully aware of how blessed we are, exercise feels like a breath of fresh air when we embrace every opportunity to exercise as a gift from God.

Precious Lord,

Thank You for the gift of my body. I will say this every day despite the many flaws I see. You have gifted me with a measure of health, and I will use it for Your glory. I want to take care of the good things I've been given so I can give You a great return on Your investment in me. As I pursue a greater level of physical health, keep me close to Your heartbeat. I want to keep things in perspective, and I want to honor You in everything I do. Thank You for loving me the way You do. I love You too. Amen.

Steps Toward Health

- I will take an honest assessment of my current fitness level by consulting with a health professional who can develop a fitness plan to fit my needs (absolutely worth the money if you can manage it).
- I will write down some tangible, doable goals to be accomplished over the next four weeks.
- I will resist the temptation to compare myself with others, or even with a level of fitness I attained years ago.
- When I'm tempted to avoid working out, I will call a friend and ask her to walk with me.
- I will not entertain thoughts that weaken or defeat me. I will put my hope in the Lord.

Try This

- Get a physical. Let your doctor know about your exercise plans and follow his or her advice.
- Decide what kind of exercise you want to do, and then invest in a good pair of shoes appropriate for that activity. The right shoes are *extremely important* for protecting your joints.
- Here's an easy way to keep track of your exercise: Put a small *o* on your calendar on the days you get cardio exercise; put a small *x* on the days you do strength work. This will not only help keep you accountable, but will also give you a realistic perspective of how often you're exercising. Typically, it's good to do

strength work two to three times per week, and cardio exercise three to five times per week. For some, this may feel like a lofty goal. Always remember, something is better than nothing.

- There's absolutely no need to exercise seven days a week. In fact, it's better for your body to have days of rest and recovery. Your body needs time to repair and heal. Just as you mark your calendar for exercise, consider marking your calendar for rest and recovery. Don't fill up that extra space with a busyness that drains you. Make some time and space to rest in a way that nourishes you. Take an Epsom salt bath. Go to bed early. Put on some music, put your head back, and pray. (More on rest— the most underrated discipline of all—later.)

- If you cannot afford a health club membership, consider renting a piece of equipment for your home. Some places will allow you to rent-to-own. When my kids were very young, I rented a treadmill during the winter months and exercised while they were napping.

- If renting a piece of equipment is out of the question, consider purchasing a couple of exercise videos or seeing if your local library has some to check out. One of the videos should give you more than 20 minutes of cardio (aerobic exercise), and the other one should work your muscles. Make sure these videos give more than a couple of minutes to stretching at the end of your workout. While I am sure countless good videos are out there, try to purchase videos instructed by someone who holds a certification in fitness. Just because someone is famous doesn't mean they know a lot about proper body mechanics.

Balance Application

Part of moving forward is taking an honest assessment of where we are now. There is no shame in this at all. In fact, it takes courage and humility to admit where we are, what we need, and where we want to go. As long as we are in Christ, we can admit our weakness and need, and then we can look up to find our strength in Him. Even in our weakness, especially in our weakness, we say out loud, "But my God is strong in me." The Lord cares about our health and wants us to be free and victorious in every area of our lives. This is my prayer for you: "Dear friend, I pray that you may prosper in every way and be in good health physically just as you are spiritually" (3 John 1:2 HCSB).

Study Time

1. Read Proverbs 16:32.

2. What are the two key virtues this verse speaks of?

3. Write down this verse in your own words, applying it to your own situation. (For example, "It's better for me to...")

4. Once more, write down this verse, but this time in prayer form. (For example, "Lord, I will be...")

5. Read Proverbs 25:28. Apply this verse to your own life. In what ways could your life be toppled without self-control?

6. Read 2 Peter 1:6.

7. Do we have enough strength in ourselves to make lasting changes in our lives? Write down your thoughts, along with a fresh declaration of dependence on God alone. Remind your soul of how *for you* He is.

8. To grow physically and spiritually, we need self-control, patient endurance, and godliness. What leads us to these attributes?

Personal Reflection

1. This week we're taking an honest look at where we are now and where we want to be. Someone once said, "If you do what you've always done, you'll get what you've always gotten." It's time for something new. What's one new life-giving habit you'd like to see emerge and even upstage what you've always done?

2. Have you identified certain people and/or scenarios that consistently tempt you to indulge, control, or overstep what God has for you? Spend some time with God on that one and ask Him what wisdom looks like here.

3. When we're determined to do something new, the devil dredges up old sins, mistakes, or missteps because he wants you looking back when you need to be looking forward. Whenever we endeavor to take new territory God has offered us, the Enemy shows up to oppose, taunt, and harass us. Stay sober, alert, and prayerful. Determine to stay the course.

This Week's Goal:

_____

_____

_____

God's Promise to Me:

_____

_____

_____

What Keeps You Balanced, Grounded?

Time with Jesus first thing in the morning.

Mostly "no" to outside things on Monday (I need to be home!). Also:

- Workout 3 times a week—45 minutes or more
- Keep in contact with my people
- Be thankful
- Laugh
- Create (I like to edit and caption photos and write)

—Kathy

Seven

Time to Move!

I can do everything through Christ, who gives me strength.
PHILIPPIANS 4:13

Many years ago, prior to this book's first release, I asked our family doctor, "What would you say is the most prevailing problem among your patients?" Without hesitating he said, "A sedentary lifestyle. Most of my patients would not need to be seen if they simply ate less and exercised more." That day as I drove home, I pondered my doctor's words. At that same moment, the radio blared with a report from the Centers for Disease Control, stating that each year in the United States, as many as 300,000 people die from obesity-related issues. Would you believe that stat is now more than 12 years old? More and more we are hearing that this issue has reached epidemic proportions and is now affecting our children.

Dr. Kristi Haertl is a professor for the Department of Occupational Science and Occupational Therapy at St. Catherine University. She's also a former fitness colleague of mine. I asked her for the latest research on obesity, especially as it relates to children. Here's what she said:

Sadly, according to the Centers for Disease Control, childhood obesity has more than tripled since the 1970s, with about 1 in 5 school-aged children (6–19) having obesity. Increasingly we are seeing programs aimed at public health and nutrition to help combat this disturbing trend. As I conducted a literature search, I found an interesting study published in *Pediatrics* in 2011 that indicated children in families that ate together (five or more meals a week), were 25 percent less likely to have nutritional issues or be overweight. A more recent study at the University of Minnesota found that the emotional tone of the meal is also important. Children who partook in family meals with patterns of hostility were more likely to be overweight or obese than those who were in a family meal that was warmer and more communicative.

These stats speak directly to the rat-race culture we live in today. We rush through our moments and our days; we take shortcuts with our food and our family time, and not without consequence. God invites us to slow down, breathe in, truly taste and enjoy our food, and create an atmosphere of faith, hope, and love for our children. These actions matter deeply on an emotional, spiritual, and physical level. Furthermore, we're made to move. And we feel so much better when we do!

Physical imbalance is a serious problem, and yet the remedy is simple: We need to eat better, eat more appropriate portions for our age and body composition (for some, that means eat more, and for others, that means eat less), and we need to get moving. Exercise is important for our health, our outlook, and our quality of life. As I mentioned earlier, it takes energy to make energy, but the payoff is worth the effort.

As we prepare to improve our lifestyle, we must also prepare ahead for those days when it would be easier to do nothing. It's easier to eat what's in front of us rather than put the time into preparing a healthy meal. It's easier to sit on the couch in front of the TV after a long, hard day, but we all know the easier path is rarely the fruitful path. The Bible says, "The slacker craves, yet has nothing, but the diligent is *fully satisfied*" (Proverbs 13:4 HCSB, emphasis added). Here are a few tips to help you prepare ahead of time for those days when you just don't feel like exercising.

- Write down your goals in a simple form and put them on your refrigerator.

- Add an element of accountability. Exercise with a friend. Your chances of canceling your workout are reduced by about 50 percent. Text each other each night and honestly share and rate your food choices.

- Make provision in your schedule for your workout ahead of time. When you go through your day hoping time won't get away from you, know that it will—every time.

- Set your watch or phone to remind you to get up and walk around for a few minutes for every hour you spend sitting at a desk. Studies show that sitting for hours at a time can negatively affect your circulation, mood, focus, and energy. It's great for your heart and for your overall well-being to get up and get moving even for five minutes on the hour.

Okay, so here we go. We've talked about physical "input"—how we nourish ourselves. Now we move on to "output"—how we respond to what's been deposited in us. We are wired to move, and the more we move, the more efficiently our bodies respond to what we're asking them to do. This chapter is filled with practical and technical advice on exercise. Refuse to be overwhelmed. Just digest a little at a time. This is good information for you to have, and knowing and applying proper technique will allow you the best results possible.

Here are the five components to fitness:

1. Cardio/respiratory endurance
2. Muscular strength
3. Muscular endurance
4. Flexibility
5. Body composition

To keep this simple and basic, we'll talk about three of them:

1. Cardio/respiratory endurance

2. Strength work (referring to both muscular strength and endurance)

3. Flexibility

Cardio/Respiratory Endurance

Cardio/respiratory endurance is measured by how our heart and lungs respond to movement. Three things affect our cardio endurance: how often we exercise, how intensely we exercise, and how long each workout lasts. Every day we set aside time for the specific purpose of getting our hearts pumping and filling our lungs with oxygen for a sustained period of time, we give our bodies the gift of these benefits:

1. Balanced "input"

2. Increased circulation

3. Strengthened heart and lung systems

4. Improved organ function

5. Improved outlook

6. Metabolized fat

7. Reduced stress

8. Improved appearance and sense of health and strength

As I travel around and speak to women, they often approach me with this question: "I'm a mom of several children. I run after them all day long. Isn't *that* exercise? And if so, why am I not losing weight?" This is an excellent question. The two forms of cardio exercise are aerobic and anaerobic. *Aerobic* basically means "in the presence of oxygen" and *anaerobic* means "without the presence of oxygen."

You may ask, "But aren't we living, breathing creatures? Aren't we always using oxygen to live?" Yes, this is true. As you sit and read this book, your body is at a certain level of *homeostasis*, meaning your input of oxygen and the demand you're placing on your body are in balance with each other. But if you were to get up and run up the stairs, your heart would start pumping, requiring an energy system to kick in. In this case your body would use the anaerobic energy system because your run upstairs required quick, accessible energy. Your body stores a certain amount of energy in your muscles ready and available for quick movement. You may have recently eaten some carbohydrates, and your body has broken them down and stored them for when you'll need them for quick use.

"Quick use" might mean dashing across the mall parking lot in the rain, rushing to the edge of your yard to keep your toddler from running into the street, or simply running after your children throughout the day. Because these activities require only stints of energy, your body uses up the carbohydrates stored in your muscles. An important note here: This is often why we get the munchies throughout the day. Our bodies want us to replenish those immediate energy stores. Where we go wrong is munching on empty calories that do little more than raise our blood sugar level to a high buzz, only to allow us to crash and burn a little later in the day. This is why I love a healthy snack bar. It provides protein, vitamins, and carbohydrates.

The anaerobic energy system has great purpose. As you can see, countless scenarios each day require quick movement. When you pick up around the house (low level of energy expended) and when you sprint across the parking lot (high level of energy expended for a short time), you tap into your anaerobic system. Many sports are anaerobic in nature, like gymnastics, golf, and short sprints in track-and-field. Athletes who train in the anaerobic zone increase their threshold, and their bodies recover much more efficiently than those who are not used to that kind of exercise.

I'm writing to the average person who is not a trained athlete. To burn fat, work out longer, and recover in a more enjoyable fashion, you need to work out in the aerobic zone. In other words, you need a nice, slow warm-up that sends your body the message, "I am warming up slowly. I am going to be out here for a while, and I need oxygen to help me." Just a note about the warm-up: When we start working out too quickly without a proper warm-up, we tell our bodies, "There's no way I can possibly sustain this pace for a long period of time, so I probably won't need any oxygen." Our nervous system reads that message, and suddenly we find ourselves breathing hard, needing to slow way down, and wondering if we are even cut out for this exercise thing.

Once you begin a nice, slow warm-up, you will feel your heart rate gradually increase. Give yourself time to get used to it, and then little by little, increase your intensity until you're breathing hard but can still carry on a conversation. When you hit the "zone," you'll notice you have arrived at a new level of balance or homeostasis. In other words, the demand you're putting on your body is met with the necessary oxygen to fulfill the task. Isn't that amazing?

This is where it gets fun. On average, it takes about 20 minutes of this kind of sustained exercise to efficiently burn fat.[1] If you're generally healthy, a 30–60-minute cardio workout, several times a week, is a great goal. This is not a hard-and-fast rule, but more of a generic scale. Each person is different, and each of us will access oxygen either quickly or slowly, depending on our current fitness level. The more fit you are, the quicker you will be able to warm up, access oxygen, and recover afterward. When you take the time to invest in your health, your body pays you back in great dividends.

Here are a few things to remember:

1. Exercise on an empty stomach or after a light snack.
2. Drink plenty of water before, during (if possible), and after exercise. Muscles work better when they are hydrated, and drinking water is like "internal" exercise.
3. Give yourself five to seven minutes to warm up.
4. Listen to your body and push just beyond what you feel like doing.
5. Give yourself five to ten minutes to cool down.
6. Always gently stretch after exercising.

Strength Work

Muscular strength refers to the amount of weight you can lift. *Muscular endurance* refers to how many repetitions you can complete. To keep it simple, muscular strength asks "how much" and muscular endurance asks "how long." When we regularly invest some of our time building strong, lean muscles, these are the benefits we enjoy:

1. Supported frame
2. Minimized risk of injury
3. Increased circulation
4. Improved outlook
5. Increased levels of strength
6. Increased metabolism (which helps us burn fat more efficiently)
7. Increased physical freedom
8. Improved appearance and sense of health and strength

A point to remember: *heavy objects either injure us or make us stronger*. Every single day someone is injured from either lifting improperly or moving an object too heavy for them. Proper strength work strengthens our frames and lessens our chance of injury. Strength work consists of exercises that tone your muscles. You can use weights or your own body weight as a form of resistance. It's supremely important that you not only talk with your doctor before engaging in resistance training, but that you use proper form and technique for every single strength exercise. Countless people injure themselves because they either don't know what they're doing or they've grown so comfortable with their routine that they've stopped paying attention to the importance of engaged muscles and good form. Here are a few suggestions:

- Seek out a personal trainer or group fitness class at a reputable fitness center. (Important note: Not all health clubs are the same.)

- Go to YouTube and type in "proper squats" or "proper pushups" and you'll not only view proper technique, but you'll find other exercise suggestions as well.

- Check out my friend Ashley Darkenwald's book *Living Wellness for Growth Groups*. She offers balanced diet and exercise advice as well as pictures that show proper form for the most popular strength exercises (and she incorporates a faith perspective).

As we regularly engage in physical resistance training, our strength limitations break down. Then as we recover, we rebuild and arrive at a new threshold that gives us an increased capacity for lifting, pushing, and pulling. We are so fearfully and wonderfully made!

To grow, we must push beyond what is comfortable, which requires effort and energy. That is why it's important to give our muscle groups a day of recovery after working them. Let me say again that proper technique is of paramount importance. The slightest rotation of a body part could make all the difference between working the muscle and injuring the joint. That is why you want to seek instruction from one who knows about proper alignment.

> To grow, we must push beyond what is comfortable, which requires effort and energy.

As I mentioned earlier, if you belong to a reputable health club, the personal trainers there should be able to walk you through a list of good strength exercises and proper form. As you stay consistent with your strength work, you will carry yourself differently, you will feel better, and you will enjoy more physical freedom.

Building muscle, as I mentioned above, will also change your metabolism. That's right; you can change your metabolism! If you have a slow metabolism, engage in a thorough and safe strength work routine about two to four times per week, and you will enjoy noticeable changes in no time. A fitness friend recently told me that if you build a few pounds of muscle into your frame, you will burn significantly more fat each year. As your muscle density increases, so will your metabolism.

Flexibility

Flexibility is determined by the range of motion you have around each joint. This is probably the most neglected component of exercise. Many people are vigorous in their cardio and strength workouts, only to skip stretching afterward. People have told me stretching takes too much time. You can get away with this for a while, but eventually muscles (especially developing ones) will get tighter and tighter, which is a recipe for injury. Most injuries require a time of rest, which can push you all the way back to where you started. So invest some time in stretching. It is essential.

When you stretch, avoid bouncing. Make sure your stretches are gentle and deliberate. If you ask your body to stretch too far too soon, your muscles will rebound and you may injure yourself. As with every other component of fitness, take small, consistent steps. I deal with a lot of regular pain due to my problematic joint issues. I have learned that every time my body begins to ache, I need to spend some extra time stretching. I would venture to say that most of our aches and pains would be eliminated if we stretched regularly. Here are a few things to remember:

- *Don't stretch cold muscles.* Begin your workout with a proper warm-up (we call it a warm-up because that's exactly what it's for—to get the blood flowing and moving to your muscles). Studies show injuries can occur when we stretch before we've properly warmed up. It's better to do a thorough, deep stretch at the end of your workout. However, doing basic range of motion movements without a workout is better than not doing them at all. Just don't stretch your muscles when they're cold. Move first, then stretch.

- *Don't hold your breath when stretching.* Keep your breathing steady. Breathe in through the nose and out through the mouth.

- *Hold your stretches for at least 20 seconds* (20-30 seconds is ideal). If your muscle starts to rebound or pull back, release the stretch and next time don't pull quite as far.

Tangible Tips for Exercise

Choose your workout days. Talk to family members and decide which days you'll work out each week. It's much easier to stay consistent if your schedule doesn't vary too much.

Choose your cardio mode. It doesn't matter whether you're walking, running, taking an aerobics class, or following an exercise video. Just plan ahead of time and stick to it. (The "I'll figure it out when I get there" mind-set is never as effective.)

Balance your strength work. It's best to work opposing muscle groups in the same workout. Most aerobics classes and videos are designed this way. If you are working out on your own, think of it this way: If you work biceps, work your triceps; if you work your chest, work your back; if you work your quadriceps (upper thigh), work your hamstrings (back upper leg). Working opposing muscle groups will keep you balanced and strong. If you ever see a muscle-bound body builder who hovers over his bulging pectoral (chest) muscles, know that he most likely has not done enough back work or proper stretching. We can pull our bodies out of alignment if we work one muscle group without working the other.

Change things up occasionally. Because our bodies are so adaptable, they will adjust to the consistent messages we send them. This works in our favor for a while because our systems become more efficient. Where this can work against us, though, is when we hit a plateau. If we fall into the rut of doing the same thing all the time, we cease to be challenged and need to introduce something new into our routine. This is why cross training is so effective. Challenge your system by throwing in a different mode of exercise. You can also change your usual workout by increasing the intensity or length of your workout. This will give your body an athletic edge and keep you from falling into a rut.

Make time for stretching. This bears repeating: Set aside a little time for stretching. You will feel wonderful afterward, and you'll greatly reduce your risk of injury. Even ten minutes at the end of your workout—which adds up to only 40 minutes per week—will change how you feel and how you respond to exercise.

Don't make decisions while running uphill. I learned this the hard way, but the lesson is a good one. Whether you're at the hard part in your workout, a hard part of your day, or even struggling in a difficult time in life, don't decide what your goals are (or aren't) or how far you will be able to go (or not). Wait until you level out and you're breathing regularly before you honestly make any assessment.

Know that your disciplines will carry you—for a while. But only for a while. Once you get into a groove, your body will get better and better at responding to what you're asking it to do. What's wonderful is that you can have an off day or two and step out of your routine while still enjoying the benefits of your past disciplines. But this will go only so far. If your "off days" become the rule rather than the exception, your body will then begin to read those messages and respond accordingly. Do your best not to let your diet and exercise routine get away from you by more than a few days. Again, remember, if you are in a short-term crisis, exercise will be the furthest thing from your mind. If you are in a long-term crisis, you will *need* to keep your strength up by taking care of yourself. It is one of the smartest things you can do.

For some, the whole diet and exercise thing may seem way out of reach. If you feel this way, try the following easy steps, which, I pray, will help you change the momentum in your life.

Ten Steps in Ten Weeks to Tiptoe Toward a Healthy Lifestyle

Add one discipline at a time while continuing the previous ones.

Week 1: Drink eight to ten glasses of water daily.

Week 2: Add one vegetable a day to your diet.

Week 3: Commit to ten minutes of exercise two to four times this week (for example, stretch, walk, do sit-ups).

Week 4: Rid yourself of a bad habit—and work to keep it out of your life. (Remember, maintenance is easier than gaining lost ground.)

Week 5: Add one fruit a day to your diet.

Week 6: Increase the length of your workout by 10 to 15 minutes.

Week 7: Add another vegetable to your daily diet.

Week 8: Change your "indulgence" rule. Whether you overindulge in sweets, breads, or fried foods, make yourself abide by a more disciplined rule (for example, limit sweets or fried foods to weekends only).

Week 9: Quit eating after dinner and before bed (or at least change the rule to weekends only).

Week 10: Assess your progress and make any necessary adjustments. For example, if you're still eating too much or not exercising enough, do your best to bring balance in these areas.

Dear Lord,

I am thankful that nothing is too hard for You, not even this goal of a healthier, stronger life. I will look to You each day for strength, wisdom, and protection as I seek a more balanced and disciplined life. Help me to know when it is wise to push through the obstacles and when You are calling me to pull back a bit and just rest. You are my highest goal, not a perfectly fit body or my perfectly managed disciplines. So I will keep my eyes on You, knowing You will lead me in the way I should go. You understand me and my stage of life, and You love me. Help me to listen to everything You say to me. Amen.

Steps Toward Health

- I will thank God out loud for the many gifts He has given me.
- I will learn proper technique (and any modifications I need to make for my health) for squats, push-ups, and other resistance exercise, and I will take a few minutes this week to add some "strength" to my day.
- I will put some time into cardio exercise today.
- I will call a good friend and ask her to keep me accountable.
- I will push myself just beyond my comfort zone.

Try This

- Set a goal to work out several times per week for the next month. If you achieve this goal, treat yourself to something special. This can be very motivating!

- As you get used to your workouts, put more energy into your movements. Notice how easy it is to increase your intensity.

- When you feel unmotivated, go over your fitness goals and make yourself do *something*.

- First go to YouTube and search for a proper hamstring stretch so you can see a visual example of proper technique. If you need help with this stretch, try this: Use a towel for the stretching portion of your workout. Lie on your back and hold the ends of the towel in your hands. Straighten one of your legs and put the arch of that foot in the loop of the towel. Gently pull on the ends of the towel so that your leg comes toward you. This is a safe and effective way to stretch your hamstrings.

- Improve your posture. Whether you are sitting down or standing up, make a conscious effort to sit up straight. Pull your shoulders back and your abs in. This simple habit engages muscles that help support your frame. Plus, it takes pounds off your appearance.

Balance Application

At first this information may seem overwhelming, but in time it will become second nature. As you do the exercises, you'll begin to notice when something doesn't feel right. Pay attention to how you're feeling. If you're struggling because it's difficult, that's okay; make yourself exercise anyway. But if a certain joint feels unstable or you're experiencing unusual pain, then be sure to stop and talk to your doctor. Usually when someone buys an expensive piece of equipment, they take the time to read the manual so they can get the best use from it and not damage the equipment because of their lack of knowledge. As you learn the basic mechanics of movement, you'll be able to do effective strength work in your living room, out on your deck, or even in a hotel room. Give yourself room to grow and learn, and you'll experience the great satisfaction of having a healthy, strong body.

Study Time

1. Read 1 Corinthians 9:26-27. In what ways is God calling you to discipline your body? What steps will you take to move in that direction?

2. Does the thought of incorporating a regular exercise program intimidate or overwhelm you?

3. Read Philippians 4:13. Read it again and meditate on this promise.

4. Write out a personalized prayer of faith, incorporating this verse.

5. Read 1 Timothy 4:8.

6. What is far more important than exercising our physical bodies?

7. What kind of season are you in with the Lord right now?

8. Pause and ask the Lord to draw you deeper with Him. Pray for your loved ones.

Personal Reflection

1. This week we're learning more about the importance of good technique and steady application. God wired our bodies for strength and movement, and He is with us on this journey. Spend some time thanking God for all that's right with your health. For example, *Thank You, Lord, for my digestive system—that I can eat and digest foods. Thank You, Lord, that I have eyes to see and ears to hear, and a heart to do Your will.*

2. What aspect of fitness and exercise intrigues you most?

Strength work? Cardio exercise? Flexibility? Ask God for not only the capacity to learn what you need to know, but also for the motivation to apply what He teaches you. This is not a trivial pursuit. He cares about you, and He cares about your health.

3. Do you see a spiritual connection to your physical condition? Really think about this one. If God is calling you to build up your physical strength, might He also be asking you to shore up your faith? Or if He's inviting you to work on flexibility, might He also be asking you to move out of your comfort zone? Write down your thoughts.

This Week's Goal:

_____

_____

_____

God's Promise to Me:

_____

_____

_____

What Keeps You Balanced, Grounded?

Start and end every day with Scripture. In particular, I pray Psalm 91 and Ephesians 6—out loud—at the beginning and ending of every day. Quiet time with family is key. We just talk, without the interruption of computers or media of any sort. We've learned to also pay attention in these talks, and just being there to listen is sometimes the best thing we can do. Board games are fun. We've learned the value of turning off the TV and turning on the music. Also, a daily walk for even ten minutes is awesome for balance. My advice? Slow down, read to learn, and grow. Finally, life is great when you really learn to rest in the Lord.

—Jan

Eight

Too Busy to Rest?

It's useless to rise early and go to bed late, and
work your worried fingers to the bone. Don't you
know he enjoys giving rest to those he loves?
PSALM 127:2 MSG

When my sons were babies, I battled a disease and tried desperately to keep it all together.

For the first three years of his life, my youngest child got up every
other hour. I received all kinds of advice on getting him to sleep, and
none of it worked. Added to my lack of consistent sleep were a toddler
and a preschooler who *had* gotten a good night's sleep. They were ready
to party at the break of dawn!

Another factor that immensely complicated this stage of life was
the battle going on inside my body. Lyme disease stole every ounce
of energy I had. I experienced countless scary neurological symptoms
while trying to care for my three little ones. My poor husband worked
two—sometimes three—jobs and spent every free moment caring for
our busy household. He carried a weight of worry for our finances, my
health, and our future. By the time his head hit the pillow at night,
he snored rhythmically. Most nights I tried to let him get his much-
needed rest.

One night in bed, feeling desperate for rest, I started to doze into a slumber. My whole body felt as if it were falling into a hole that pulled me from my senses. Oh, how I needed this! I was about to be carried away into a deeper sleep when I heard an annoying beep, beep, beep sound. It was the middle of the night, and I thought, *Who would set their alarm and ruin my life this way?* (Thoughts of a desperate woman...) My head seemed to weigh a hundred pounds as I lifted it off the pillow and looked for the alarm. I realized in seconds that it wasn't an alarm; it was my little baby crying at the top of his lungs. Again. He was sick and coughing up a storm. I dragged my heavy limbs out of bed and into his bedroom. Truly, if a heart could stop beating from sheer exhaustion, I knew mine would. I have never known such fatigue as I did back then.

My kids are grown up and married, and I now have the time to rest and recover when I need it. As I minister to young moms and look back on my own life, another thing occurs to me. Often, because of our society's mixed-up values, young moms often feel incidental. In other words, countless messages tell them it is not enough to put their time into *just* raising their children.

Because we live in a society that constantly measures our value by what we achieve or what we produce, many young moms feel the pressure to be involved in far too many pursuits—more than God would ever ask of them. I was once one of those young, overcommitted moms; now I am older and deeply burdened for moms who are distracted, depleted, and completely exhausted.

If anyone ever had an excuse or reason to do only one thing at church, it's a young mother. If anyone has a need for physical and mental rest, it's a young mother. How different it would be for her if she decided to use what little extra time she has to get replenished. At times, that could mean a nap. Other times, it could mean a bubble bath, going out to eat, or going to bed early. I know and understand the need for some to have an interest outside the home. To many of us, that sort of thing is a saving grace, but there is a difference between doing *some*thing and doing five things. I even understand the desire to have a lot of girlfriend connection during this stage of life; one can only talk to toddlers about potty chairs and sippy cups for so long. But still, I'd venture to say that young moms would feel better if they put a higher priority on getting the rest their bodies so desperately need and on spending time with the One who can truly replenish their souls.

Just a little side note: If you're tired of caring so much about what others think of your schedule, or if you have a difficult time saying no and you long to break free from all the unappointed ought-to's and should-do's, I'd love for you to check out my book *Your Sacred Yes: Trading Life-Draining Obligations for Freedom, Passion, and Joy.* I believe it'll equip and encourage you greatly!

Rest Is Hard to Come By

This problem doesn't stop with young moms. Women in all seasons of life juggle countless responsibilities and busy schedules. My dear mama is in her mid-eighties, and she is just as busy as the rest of us. A few weeks ago several of my siblings and I communicated back and forth on a group text. We'd somehow talked ourselves into a worst-case scenario. None of us had heard from our mom that morning, and she wasn't answering her phone. One of my sisters finally texted, "That's it. I'm going over there to find out if she's okay." We all waited anxiously to hear from our sister. About 40 minutes later Krissy texted us back, "She's not dead. She's just booked solid today. Her day-calendar is open on the counter here and she's swamped with activities from morning until evening!" We all laughed at our own ability to create a phantom catastrophe, and we scolded our mom for not running her schedule by us. (Ha-ha. Well, we tried to pull off that one, but she's got a mind of her own.)

It seems that our culture lends itself to this kind of lifestyle. Our fast-paced society puts such a low value on rest and recovery that some think rest is only for the weak. The truth is rest is *as big* a component to health and fitness as diet and exercise. Since God calls us—even commands us—to rest, He will provide a way for us. Here are a few of the many side effects of a life without rest:

• Weakened immune system

- Loss of perspective
- Interrupted healing process
- More injuries
- Increased mental strain
- Increased risk of error, misjudgment, and mistakes
- Increased strain on relationships
- Balance is not possible

An old chiropractor friend once shared some amazing insight on the issue of rest. He said most of his female patients who struggle with chronic fatigue syndrome and fibromyalgia have a common thread issue in their lives: interrupted, inconsistent sleep. Whether it's from living near an airport, sleeping next to a snoring husband, or getting up with a baby, these women are exhausted. However, their health would greatly improve if they could get a consistent night's sleep.

He further explained the sleep cycle to me, which was fascinating. Did you know our bodies supply a necessary growth hormone *only* when we hit that fourth stage of the sleep cycle, and we should typically go through this cycle about three to four times every night? He further explained, "This hormone provides our bodies with something like 'little wrenches.' We need these to build us back up, because every day we injure ourselves (daily wear and tear) and every night we need to heal. When our bodies don't get the benefits of that fourth stage of sleep, our health breaks down."

Is it even possible to go against the flow of the insane pace of this world and provide ourselves with consistent rest? Yes! Absolutely. First, we need to let go of the lie that says, "Rest is an optional, moveable component in my life" and replace it with the truth that says, "Rest replenishes my body, heals my body, and helps me feel my best. God calls me to rest in whatever season I am in, and He will help me find it."

> We need to let go of the lie that says, "Rest is an optional, moveable component in my life."

Just as we need to eat better and exercise more efficiently, we need to make sure we get consistent, quality rest. That may sound silly, especially to young moms, but we have both scientific and biblical proof that rest must not be optional. Your efforts may be inconsistent at best, but making rest a high priority in your life will help you do more than just survive a demanding schedule. A heart at rest brings peace to the home. There is no virtue in being worn-out all the time.

This gets at the core of what we believe. If we *really* believe that when we eat better and exercise consistently we'll feel better, have more energy, enjoy a higher quality of life, and rid ourselves of the distraction of physical imbalance—if we really believe our choices will make that much of a difference—we will believe God for a better pace and apply ourselves to those disciplines.

Many of us could put a higher value on our need for a healthy diet, exercise, and rest and then find a way to work them into our lives. Millions already do so every single day. I've heard stories of people committed to staying healthy and fit and yet were too poor for a club membership or even exercise equipment. They didn't let a lack of finances stop them. They filled milk jugs with sand and used them for weights. They rigged pulleys in their basements and created their own equipment. They believed the benefits of these choices outweighed their many legitimate excuses, and they *found a way*. It's the same with rest. When you start to notice how your perspective improves, how your joy returns, and how much better food energizes you when you are rested, you'll protect your need for rest because you'll come to believe God when He says rest will bless you.

Pay Attention to What You Really Need

I woke up one Saturday morning, went through my morning routine, and tried to psych myself up for the lengthy list of chores with my name on it. But for some reason I just couldn't get my day off the ground. I was exhausted and lacked the peace and clarity I usually enjoy. My boys were all gone for the day, and I found my way up to my bedroom and turned on the TV. I was just going to watch for a *little bit*, and then I would tackle the mountain of laundry that awaited me.

Before I knew it, I had wasted four and half hours watching movies! I peeled myself out of my bed and went downstairs to a pile of dishes in the sink, food wrappers on the counter, and my laundry still sitting there. On top of it all, that unsettled feeling in my soul was still with me. I was so mad at myself. I had squandered a perfectly good afternoon. Later that evening I went to the living room to pray. I asked the Lord for forgiveness for wasting the day and spent time with Him until He showed me what was really bothering me.

I lacked peace that morning because I had let my mind wander back to old worries and anxious thoughts. Instead of confessing my fears and replacing them with God's truth, I stuffed them down below the surface. Those unresolved fears hung heavy in my soul that morning and kept me from true joy. Instead of immediately finding my rightful place of peace with God, I found my way up to my bed and laid mindlessly in front of the TV—which did nothing for me. I sat in my living room realizing I lost my peace because I lost sight of Him. So I bowed my head and focused once again on His immeasurable love for me. I got right with Him and sensed His forgiveness, direction, and a fresh dose of mercy.

Well, months later, a similar but different situation occurred. I had just finished an intense speaking engagement. My family welcomed me home, and we enjoyed connecting with one another again. I unpacked, did the laundry, and caught up on tasks around the house. The following day was Sunday, and after church all my steam left me. I was exhausted. I sat down and prayed, "I'm tired, Lord." He so clearly and sweetly said to me, *Go lie down and watch a movie.*

You might find this odd, as did I. My boys were gone for the afternoon, and Kevin was busy in the den, so I snuggled in bed with a book and the remote. I didn't watch a movie, but I did watch the news and read a book during the commercials. I thoroughly enjoyed myself, and when I got up, I felt rested and replenished. What was different this time? I thought through both scenarios and learned a powerful lesson.

God is gracious and gives us room to eat good food, watch fun movies, and spend time doing what we enjoy. But here's a critical point: When we turn to food, movies, and hobbies when we *lack peace and intimacy with God*, we're drinking from "cracked cisterns" (Jeremiah 2:13). A cracked cistern is a broken well and a source far beneath God's best for us.

Read the powerful verse below, but before you do, think about a time when you intentionally chose to medicate yourself with something less than God. Now imagine the surprise of the heavenly hosts, unable to comprehend how any of us could settle for anything less than what has been made available to us.

> "Has any nation ever traded its gods for new ones, even though they are not gods at all? Yet my people have exchanged their glorious God for worthless idols! The heavens are shocked at such a thing and shrink back in horror and dismay," says the LORD. "For my people have done two evil things: They have abandoned me—the fountain of living water. And they have dug for themselves cracked cisterns that can hold no water at all!" (Jeremiah 2:11-13).

We all choose things over intimacy with Christ. We choose food, shopping, gossip, TV, and so on. We even choose His *gifts* over a love affair with *Him*. And yet He still loves us, still waits patiently for us, and longs for us to understand all we have in Him. The goal here is to abide so closely with the Lord that you *know* when to rest, when to exercise, when to serve, when to pray, and when it's okay just to relax and enjoy the blessings He has given you.

Precious Father,

Thank You for Your gracious love. You have the world on Your shoulders and yet You know how to rest and be at peace. You paid a high price so I could live a life of peace. Help me, Lord, to bring my life into a rhythm that honors

*You and blesses me. I know there is a way to get the rest
I need. Please help me find it. I will look to You to show me
the way I should go, each and every day and night. I love
You, Lord. Amen.*

Steps Toward Health

- If I am currently imbalanced in the area of rest, I will pray and ask God to show me what has to change so I can get more rest.

- If I drink too many caffeinated beverages, I will cut back this week.

- If I am involved in too many pursuits, I will write them down, pray about them, talk them over with a trusted friend, and then decide what has to go.

- I will set an honorable timeline for myself to step out of commitments I know God did not call me to.

- I will determine to honor and protect my God-given call to rest.

- I will determine to turn off my screens each day at a reasonable time so I can engage with my loved ones and transition out of the workday and into God's appointed time of rest and replenishment.

Try This

- *Rest from exercise too.* Our need for rest also applies to recovery time from exercise. If you have had an intense workout, give yourself the necessary time to recover. Your organs, your muscles, and your joints all need time to recoup from what you've asked them to do. Listen to your body.

- *Resist the gung-ho mentality.* Once you get going on an exercise program, it's easy to get carried away and do too much up front. Pace yourself and give yourself days off when you don't exercise at all.

- *Routine, routine, routine.* This is essential to living a life with balance, rhythm, and proper rest. Our bodies require a sense of consistency (although, as mentioned earlier, in fitness it's good to break up your routine occasionally so you don't plateau). Granted, certain stages of life make routine seem like a heroic feat; and that is just what it is. Your body will treat you like a hero if you honor its need for consistency, especially at night. Here are a few suggestions for a bedtime routine:
    - *Read a book.* If the news stresses you out, read a heartwarming story.
    - *Drink nighttime herbal tea.* Many tea options are available. Find one that settles you down without making you groggy.
    - *Take a hot Epsom salt bath.* I love Dr Teal's Epsom Salts because they come with essential oils. My favorites are lavender and eucalyptus spearmint. Put about a pound of salts in your bath and soak for at least 20 minutes. These soaks are great for detox and to transition from work to rest. Warm baths in the evening will soothe your muscles and slow down your heart rate.
    - *Don't lie down more than an hour before bed (unless you're dealing with adrenal fatigue or some other chronic illness, in which case the extra rest will do you good).* However, lying down to read a book for an hour prior to bed is an excellent way to transition from work to rest. Here's the point: If you transition from dinner to the couch and spend the evening there, you may affect the quality of your sleep. If possible, take some time after dinner to go for a leisurely evening walk or bike ride. Do some laundry and dishes. Engage in some movement after dinner, and then purposely transition to your "rest" phase of the evening.
    - *Stay away from sugar and caffeinated beverages.* At least consider no sugar or soda from lunchtime on. This affects sleep for many people.

- *Guard your mind at night.* Refuse to do what my husband calls "contemplate the universe." Don't let your thoughts wander to what worries you or makes you anxious. You can't do anything about it in the middle of the night anyway. Pray yourself to sleep with statements of faith like, *"Lord, I know You care about... Thank You that You are there for me. I give You my concern over... I thank You ahead of time for a good night of rest."*

As we wrap up the section on our physical bodies, let's look at how a life out of balance affects our physical health. Just a note: In the effects listed below, "input" refers mainly to physical nourishment. "Output" refers mainly to physical exercise. "Rest" refers to recovery from exercise, from the demands of life, and mostly to a good night's sleep.

Effects of Physical Imbalance

✓ *Too much input, not enough output:* overweight, lack of energy, increased risk of disease, injury, and depression (Extreme cases: obesity-related diseases)

✓ *Too much output, not enough input:* undernourished, increased risk of illness and injury, tend to be weak in relationships (Extreme cases: anorexia and health-related issues)

  (Important note: Too much input and too much output both result in an increased risk of injury.)

✓ *Too much rest:* atrophy sets in, muscles get soft, strength is swallowed up by weakness (Better said: Rest in itself is a good thing, but too much sedentary living equals weakness and loss.)

✓ *Too little rest:* weakened immunities, bodily systems breakdown, vulnerable to sickness and disease, loss of perspective, increased risk of injury, loss of strength

(Important note: Too much rest and too little rest both result in a loss of strength.)

Balance Application

Rest is so important. Our bodies need to heal, and we need to be replenished from exercise, events, busy weeks, and hard conversations. A counselor once told me it takes our nervous system 48 hours to return to its natural state after a painful conversation. If it takes our divinely wired nervous systems time to recover when pushed beyond their normal boundaries, how much more do our minds, our hearts, our joints, and our muscles need to rest and recover from the constant demands of life? We even need to allow our digestive system a time to rest from food. It's important to pay attention to the needs of our bodies and souls. Rest is a beautiful thing. God-directed rest will replenish and renew us.

Study Time

1. Read the following verse: "My soul finds rest in God; my salvation comes from him" (Psalm 62:1 NIV).

2. If we can trust God with our eternity, we can trust Him with every lesser thing. What thoughts often interrupt your time of rest? Write them down.

3. Look again at what you've written down. Has the Enemy used any threats, lies, and fears on you that now seem familiar?

4. Read Philippians 4:6-7. Read it again, and again, and again. Memorize it and do what it says.

5. Read Hebrews 4:10-11. According to the Word, what happens in a life without rest? Write it down.

6. Read Jesus's words in Mark 6:31. With what ways is He calling you to this place?

7. Will you listen to Him? How?

You are His very precious treasure. Everything you do matters to Him because He loves you.

> Didn't you realize that your body is a sacred place, the place of the Holy Spirit? Don't you see that you can't live however you please, squandering what God paid such a high price for? The physical part of you is not some piece of property belonging to the spiritual part of you. God owns the whole works. So let people see God in and through your body (1 Corinthians 6:19-20 MSG).

Personal Reflection

1. This week we're learning about the importance of quality, consistent rest. Think and pray about this aspect of your life. Write out your thoughts and a prayer, asking God for divine direction and help so your God-given rest becomes one of the sweetest gifts you enjoy.

2. What adjustments are within your power to start making today? What aspects of rest are motivating to you (for example, a more consistent bedtime, regularly using Epsom salt baths, time with a book before bed, the challenge to turn off your screens at the same time every day)?

3. I asked this question in the last chapter, but I'd like to apply it to rest this time. Do you see a spiritual connection to your physical condition? Really think about this one. Do you know how to rest physically? And how about spiritually? Read Psalm 91:1 and write down your thoughts.

This Week's Goal:

_____

_____

_____

God's Promise to Me:

_____

_____

_____

What Keeps You Balanced, Grounded?

I try to get eight hours of sleep each night. I pray every day. And read the Bible every day. I eat mostly life-sustaining kinds of foods. I love to spend time with my wife and son. I regularly exercise. I spend a few days a week volunteering my skills. And I've learned that I have to make life happen, not just wait for it to happen to me.

–Ron

Part Two

Spiritual Health

Physical training is good, but training for godliness is much better, promising benefits in this life and in the life to come.

1 Timothy 4:8

Nine

God Enjoys You

The glory of GOD—let it last forever!
Let GOD enjoy his creation!
PSALM 104:31 MSG

I really like my kids. I mean, I love them intensely, but I also really, really like them. My oldest son, Jake, is married and about ready to start a family of his own, but for many years when he lived at home, he had the most wonderful habit. That boy could not walk by me in the house without wrapping his arm around me, kissing the top of my head, and sweetly saying, "Hi, Mama" or "I love you, Mom." He is passionate and sensitive and, most importantly, he has a sincere heart for the things of God. He wandered from the faith for a season, but even then, he never stopped pursuing us, being kind and respectful to us, and engaging us in deep (sometimes painful) conversations. In fact, his hard questions about church and faith compelled me to dig deeper into why I believe what I believe. His honest journey certainly made me a better Christian. He's really one of my dearest friends. I like him so much.

Then there's my youngest son, Jordan. He's the messiest eater I've ever known, and he leaves a trail wherever he goes. He's also generous and kind and often surprises us with his sideways sense of humor. I remember such a day, many years ago. He walked up to me, placed his hands on my shoulders as if he had something very important to say, and started with, "Mom, I've decided I don't like clowns." Just as quickly he turned around and started to walk away. When I laughed and asked him why, he looked over his shoulder and said, "Anyone *that* happy is bound to turn on you!"

When Jordan lived at home, we loved to play Ping-Pong. We were pretty evenly matched back then, but whenever I'd pull ahead by several points, he'd break out into this dance. He'd hop on one foot, then the other, while flailing his arms with every swing of the paddle. I'd start to laugh and couldn't stop. He'd win every time. He was a pretty decent athlete in high school. I loved to watch him play football and basketball—loved to watch him interact with his teammates. He's married now, and I love any moment I get to spend time with him and his darling wife. He makes me laugh every time I see him. I really like my Jordan.

Luke is my middle son, and if you've ever heard me speak, you've heard me tell many stories about this one. He is now a gentle giant of a man, and a wonderful, godly husband. But he used to be a feisty, strong-willed child who spent more time in the corner than anywhere else. He and I laugh together now about those days. He thinks he should receive a share of my speaking fees since he's supplied me with much of my material.

Along with his strong-willed, feisty side, Luke also possessed the most unassuming nature. It's as though it never occurred to him to care what others might be thinking about him. One day while dressing for preschool, he asked if *he* could pick out his whole outfit. We headed for the car with Luke wearing his younger brother's too-short, too-tight shorts and a too-large, long-sleeved shirt *covered by* a small, tight T-shirt. Imagine. But that wasn't the worst of it. As he marched out to the car, each footstep made a different sound because he had a dress shoe on one foot and a snowmobile boot on the other.

When he was about five and we were planning his birthday party, Luke listed every person he wanted to invite. One of the names on his list was Bob Ziedler. What's funny about that is Bob was our friend and in his thirties at the time. But Bob always had time for Luke, and Luke wanted him at his party. So Luke's party list consisted of several five-year-olds and one thirty-year-old—and he thought nothing of it.

I'm going to tell you one more story, and trust me, there is a point to all this. Back when Luke was about eight or nine years old, we signed him up for afterschool karate. He was absolutely adorable in his little uniform. I watched him from the side of the gym. The kids were all lined up waiting for personal instruction on proper form from their instructor. Several of the boys toward the end of the line got antsy while waiting, so they took turns running to throw themselves into a mat attached to a wall, falling to the floor and laughing.

Luke was about fifth from the back of the line and enjoyed watching the boys. A couple of them noticed him and asked, "Why don't you try it?" Luke paused, and they said, "C'mon. Ya chicken?" Luke took in a deep breath, ran hard, and threw himself into the mat with all the strength he had. At that precise moment the instructor looked up and noticed Luke was out of line. He stood up, yelled at Luke, asked him what he was thinking, and made an example out of him. Luke's cheeks were bright red with embarrassment. The other boys quietly giggled while Luke stood alone.

I was overcome with affection for my son. I knew he shouldn't have stepped out of line the way he did, but I saw the whole thing. I knew what part was his, and we would talk about that later. But I also knew he felt embarrassed and exposed, and I cared far more about how the whole scenario made him feel about himself than I did about his getting out of line. More than anything I wanted him to know how much I loved him.

Comprehending the Incredible Love of God

It's just like that with God—even more so.

If I, being a sinful, selfish human being, have the capacity to cherish my boys in this way and to see the bigger picture in their lives, how much more does a loving God care for us? God loves you. He is holy and powerful. He sees when you've been set up and knows when you've been overlooked. He never looks away, He always hears you, and He listens to what is on your heart. He fully enjoys you, and it pleases His heart so much when you take the leap of faith to believe that someone as wonderful as He—the God of the universe—would *love* to come to your party.

> God loves you. He is holy and powerful. He sees when you've been set up and knows when you've been overlooked.

Do you know what nourishes the soul? It's knowing (and believing) that we are the object of God's intimate and powerful love. This is at the core of living a healthy, balanced life. If we build our lives on any other hope, we'll be disappointed. But if we wake up every single day and remind ourselves that we are unequivocally loved, cherished, and enjoyed, it will affect how we see ourselves, how we think about others, and what we choose to do with our time.

Want to know what will change you from the inside out? You'll experience life-transforming, noticeable change when you decide to know and believe and truly understand that your name is written on the hand of Almighty God, that you're someone He sings and rejoices over, and that every time He thinks of you, it is with a pure, loving, passionate heart.

This is not to say He loves everything we do. He is concerned about our sin, yes. And He disciplines those He loves (Hebrews 12:6). But His love is never up for grabs. Nothing can separate us from His love (Romans 8:31-39). And as we walk with Him, He helps us grow as His children. He perfectly paid for our sins, and He is in the process of making us holy. What a treasured truth! Scripture says this:

> Our High Priest offered himself to God as a single sacrifice for sins, good for all time. Then he sat down in the place of honor at God's right hand. There he waits until his enemies

are humbled and made a footstool under his feet. For by that one offering he forever made perfect those who are being made holy (Hebrews 10:12-14).

When we feel tolerated at best, and unlovingly assessed at worst, we will instinctively pull inward, self-protect, and close up. Why? Because we're made for and drawn to love. Love is oxygen for our souls. Yet far too many Christians believe God simply tolerates them. And the result? They strive and strain, trying to prove themselves until they're utterly exhausted. Then they turn to counterfeit solutions to numb their disappointment and satisfy their deepest longings, only to find themselves more captive and depleted than they once were.

What we believe about God's heart for us is critical and central to living a balanced, fruitful life. And most near to His heart is that we *believe* we are the object of His love. He came to save us, not to condemn us. *We* are His reward.

So how do we come to understand such a profound truth? It's simple—by *knowing* Him. The Bible tells us that knowing the Holy One results in understanding (Proverbs 9:10). How do we come to know Him? We spend time with Him. We wait quietly in His presence. We pray often and allow Him to get a word in at least just as often. We acknowledge His presence all day long. We trust Him on the dark days and praise Him on the brighter days. To grasp His love, we must stay close to Him. He cannot be to us a vending machine, a distant relative, or a sometimes friend. If we reduce Him to such things, He will love us anyway, but we are the ones who lose.

We have an incredible capacity for God because we are His design. He made us for Himself. We live in a world full of distractions and second bests. And yet nothing will satisfy or fill us like He will. Only in His presence is our fullness of joy found (Psalm 16:11 NKJV). In His presence we find our soul's deepest needs nurtured and cared for, because no one loves us or knows what we need like He does. Consider again Proverbs 9:10, "Knowledge of the Holy One results in good judgment."

As we come to know Him more and more, we will understand Scripture more and more. We will believe that He desires to connect with us more and more. We will trust Him more and more.

In her amazing book, *Ruthless: Knowing the God Who Fights for You,* Bo Stern writes:

> The knowledge that I am completely known *and* completely loved is too wonderful. My thoughts cannot capture or contain it. God sees every detail, from my wild success to my deepest sin and sorrow, and loves me in spite of all my messes and mistakes. God's love searches for me, calls me out of hiding, and assures me that it's safe to be broken in front of Him. It's right and good to need grace...The One who made us knows us and *loves us*; He loves every single particle of us and invites us to acknowledge the grandeur of His workmanship.[1]

Why do we live like paupers in our souls when God has offered us so much? We commit to more than we have time for and then live lives at a harried, frantic pace. We trade our joy for a high level of stress. What belief makes us do that? Financially we often live beyond our means, spending money we've not yet earned. Is this because we don't trust that God is good? But when it comes to faith, most of us live far *beneath* our means. We have access to the glorious riches of God's storehouses. Study the book of Ephesians, and let your spirit be strengthened by knowing all that you possess in Christ.

Could God have possibly given us more than His Son to express His love for us? And yet He not only offered His pure and precious Son as a sacrifice for our sins, but He gave us the Holy Spirit to comfort, guide, and direct us during our journey on earth. Because of Jesus's sacrifice, we have fresh mercies awaiting us with each new day. God has even placed it in the hearts of certain people to love us. When people love us, it is a gift from God.

Every morning He paints a new sky, and every night He reveals the stars once again. He doesn't do any of these things for His health; He does them for ours. It nourishes us to be fully aware of the ways God is working around us every single day.

> Do you want more and more of God's kindness and peace? Then learn to know him better and better. For as you know him better, he will give you, through his great power, everything you need for living a truly good life: he even shares his own glory and his own goodness with us! (2 Peter 1:2-3 TLB).

My husband is over six feet tall. He weighs about...Well, never mind, but he is a large man. I always groan when he thinks we should scratch each other's back, because he has twice the acreage to cover. He is a gentle giant and possesses great strength. I can think of a few times in our first years together when I sat all snuggled in bed with a cup of tea in one hand and a book in the other. One moment I'm thoroughly enjoying myself, and the next I'm watching my book and tea launch out of my hands and into the air. In Kev's world, when he pulls back the covers to get into bed, he's just pulling back the covers to get into bed. But when he whips the covers back, he produces gale-force winds. One minute I was cozy and comfortable, the next minute I was stunned, totally uncovered, as I looked first at my book on the floor across the room, and then at my spilt tea on the floor. These incidents were always a complete surprise to my husband. He didn't know his own strength. He was simply moving in proportion to his size. He is big and strong, and when he whips the covers back without thinking much about it, he causes a minor hurricane.

But on the more important issues in life, my giant of a husband is a gentle saint. When I'm hurting, he sits down, looks me in the eyes, and listens to every word I have to say. When I can't reach something, he gets it for me; when something is too heavy, he lifts it for me; and when I am afraid, he stays by my side. So when he accidentally elbows me in the face while trying to put his arm around me, I understand that his movements are large because he is large.

Now think about the strength of God. Mountains melt like wax before Him (Psalm 97:5). At the blast of His breath the bottom of the sea can be seen (2 Samuel 22:16). When you consider the awesome strength of our Almighty God, think about this: Even though God's strength is immeasurable and unmatched, He deals *gently* with us. He doesn't muscle His way into our lives and beat us into shape. He is patient with our fears and our wounds, and He leads us at a pace He knows we can keep. If the self-restraint of God doesn't speak of His love, I don't know what does.

Look at this amazing passage from Scripture:

This I call to mind and therefore I have hope: Because of the LORD's great love we are not consumed, for his compassions never fail. They are new every morning; great is your faithfulness. I say to myself, "The LORD is my portion; therefore I will wait for him." The LORD is good to those whose hope is in him, to the one who seeks him (Lamentations 3:21-25 NIV).

Comprehending the incredible love of God has so much more to do with "being" than with "doing." For that reason, I am not going to give the usual "Steps Toward Health" or "Try This" tips in this chapter. I'm going to give you time. Take time to reflect on the fact that of all there is to know and see in this vast universe, God has set His affections on *you*. He loves you and wants to renew every part of your life.

Nourish yourself on the following verses:

I am the LORD your God, who stirs up the sea, causing its waves to roar. My name is the LORD of Heaven's Armies. And I have put my words in your mouth and hidden you safely in my hand. I stretched out the sky like a canopy and laid the foundations of the earth. I am the one who says to Israel, "You are my people!" (Isaiah 51:15-16).

Golden splendor comes from the mountain of God. He is

clothed in dazzling splendor. We cannot imagine the power of the Almighty; but even though he is just and righteous, he does not destroy us. No wonder people everywhere fear him. All who are wise show him reverence (Job 37:22-24).

The LORD is good. a strong refuge when trouble comes. He is close to those who trust in him (Nahum 1:7).

The highest angelic powers stand in awe of God. He is far more awesome than all who surround his throne. O LORD God of Heaven's Armies! Where is there anyone as mighty as you, O LORD? You are entirely faithful...Happy are those who hear the joyful call to worship, for they will walk in the light of your presence, LORD...You are their glorious strength. It pleases you to make us strong (Psalm 89:7-8,15,17).

Drawing Close to God

Do you want something God has not given you yet? Are you waiting for a certain breakthrough? Precious sister, breakthroughs are never too difficult for Him. When He makes us wait longer than we want, consider this the tender care of a Father exercising restraint until our character is developed enough to handle the blessing. What we want could be a burden. Amid our pleading, begging, and positioning ourselves, He waits like the wise, loving Father He is. Now, that's restraint.

Do you continue to doubt His love for you? You get to rise every morning to His fresh mercies. His promises have your name on them. His unshakeable character and commitment to you allows you to take Him at His word. Though His love cost Him everything, and we are so quick to forget all He's done and all He's promised to do, every day He offers us a chance to begin again. Amazing, yes?

Do you long for more of Him in your life? Do you want to draw closer and closer to Him, that He may conquer every part of your heart? Our spirits are willing, but our flesh is weak. And yet the Father moves on every prayer that asks for more of Him. He moves into the yielded areas in our lives, separating with the skill of a surgeon what is holy and what is not. He hears our passionate cry and broadens the path beneath our feet. His standard is so high and we so often fall short. He could stoop down to crush us, but He doesn't. He stoops down to make us great, and it is His pleasure to do so. What is your response to Him?

> *Precious Lamb of God,*
>
> *You are my Beloved and I am Yours. Thank You for giving me grace and mercy I can barely comprehend. You've lavished Yourself upon me, even though I will never fully understand it. Lord, help me to know Your heart. Increase my capacity to know Your love. I want You to fill every low and empty place of my life. I want every anxiety and worry replaced with joy and strength. I will not waste one more day living like a pauper when You've made me an heir. Change my heart, change my mind, and change the way I live. Help me to embrace the truth that You thoroughly enjoy me, You sing over me, and You love me with a heart that is true. I love You too. Amen.*

Balance Application

This may be the most important chapter in this book. If you forget every piece of advice, do not forget His love for you. Do not let it get away from you. To stay in the center of His will is to maintain your absolute belief in His love. All of life balances on this fact. When you know your loving Father watches over you, you know storms have their limits and serve their purpose. You notice when something fresh and new springs up in front of you. You hear when He says, "This is the way, walk ye in it" (Isaiah 30:21 KJV). When we lose sight of His love, we lose. A thousand voices and circumstances tell us otherwise, but none can compare to the One who not only told us but showed us what love is.

Beloved sister, He enjoys you. He thinks you are funny and delightful and thoughtful. He wants you set free from your fears and your past so you can be strengthened for your future. Take Him at His word—His highest desire is for you.

Study Time

1. Read Exodus 15:1-12.

2. Read it again, but this time write down every description of the Lord's mightiness and strength mentioned in each verse:

Verse 1:

Verse 2:

Verse 3:

Verse 4:

Verse 5:

Verse 6:

Verse 7:

Verse 8:

Verse 9:

Verse 10:

Verse 11:

Verse 12:

3. Now read verse 13 of the passage above.

4. He displays His strength and reveals His love. In what ways has His love ransomed you? What areas in your life still need rescuing?

5. Look again at verse 13. Where is He leading us?

6. Do you think it's possible to live in that place while tending to your life here on earth?

7. Write out verse 13 in a personalized prayer.

Personal Reflection

1. This week we're learning about the importance of really, truly, deeply believing God means it when He says He's crazy about us. I want you to be gut-level honest with your answer to this question (this one is between only you and Him): How do you *feel* God feels about you? In other words, what feels true regarding God's feelings toward you?

2. After reading this chapter and the Scriptures included, what adjustments do you need to make in your perspective of God, and of His heart for you?

   Write out a fresh perspective on God's greatness and on His affection for you.

This Week's Goal:

_____

_____

_____

God's Promise to Me:

_____

_____

_____

What Keeps You Balanced, Grounded?

I remind myself that God's design in me was not a mistake, so I then ask myself, "Am I living true to my personality type, spiritual gifts, and strengths?" For example, as an introvert, I need to put my "refreshing time" of exercise or quiet time on the calendar first. This doesn't excuse me from serving in areas that aren't my strengths—we all need to step up and pitch in to bless those in our community—but if my motivating passion is for recognition and not genuine selfless giving, it will drain me. Sometimes life's rhythms are predictable and calm, but more often than not, they are a symphony filled with tensions that don't resolve in our timing. This is not a problem to solve, but a tension to manage, and with God's help, we can live it for His glory!

—Pam

Ten

Let Him Fill You

Jesus answered, "If you knew the generosity of God and who I am, you would be asking me for a drink, and I would give you fresh, living water."

JOHN 4:10 MSG

One evening as I sat in the front row of a retreat center with my head bowed, I whispered a prayer, asking God to bless the words I was about to speak. As the host opened the weekend with announcements and my introduction, I recalled the days of fasting and prayer that had helped prepare me for this retreat. The topic was prayer, and I had done my part in the preparation of my notes, my thoughts, and, most importantly, my heart.

I loved this topic because I am passionate about prayer. For many years, prayer supplied the fuel for my fire, the water for my thirst, and the strength for my heart. I longed for these women to experience a new depth in their relationship with Jesus. I wanted them to seek Him in a more intimate way than they ever had before. I had a picture in my mind of how I wanted the weekend to go, and yet it could not happen without God's divine direction.

Tell them not to leave the well. The whisper came across my heart and made it beat faster. It was almost time for me to go up and speak, and I was caught completely off guard. Again, the still, small voice whispered, *Tell them not to leave the well.* This time I could see a picture in my mind of an old, strong well made from large stones. It was virtually untouched because around it for miles were thousands of makeshift wells, which were really just holes in the ground. I suddenly had an overwhelming sense that many of the women in the crowd had come to this retreat empty, depleted, and thirsty. I sensed that many of them, out of desperation, often turned to counterfeit sources for a quick relief from pain, loneliness, insecurity, or anger. By turning to the quick fix, they missed the greater blessing God had for them.

I found myself with a choice to make. I had one idea about how the weekend should go, and God had another. His idea, of course, was better because it was living and breathing and, well, He's God. As the host finished my introduction, I stood and headed for the podium without my notes. I had butterflies in my stomach because these women had paid me to come and speak about prayer. I had no notes in front of me, only a strong sense that God had something so important on His heart for these precious women that He needed His messenger to be vulnerable, dependent, and flexible. It could not be scripted.

For the next few days I found myself utterly dependent on the Holy Spirit's direction for every message I gave. Because I longed for security and something to hold on to, I was tempted at times to rely on the notes I brought with me. And yet by releasing that security, I saw the supernatural unfold before me.

Throughout the weekend I challenged them, "Don't leave the well. Don't be so uncomfortable with your pain that you rush to a quick fix to cover it up. In your loneliness, in your hard times, and in your waiting, stay by the well until the true, pure water comes. He will come for you; He will bring healing and a new direction for your lives." Women responded in droves. Everywhere I looked, I could see them getting right with God. They humbly brought their challenges—like anger, unforgiveness, insecurities, fears, and destructive habits—to the cross. These women dared to admit their thirst before God, which took great courage. As they waited in His presence, He met them. They allowed His living water to nourish them and wash them from their sin and satisfy their thirsty souls. The weekend became an astounding reminder of how fresh things can be when they come from the hand of God.

> Don't be so uncomfortable with your pain that you rush
> to a quick fix to cover it up.

True Nourishment

Remember, we must regularly push beyond what is comfortable if we want to grow. This is especially true in our spiritual lives. If we stay too long in our comfort zones, we get a false sense of security and a distorted picture of how we're really doing. It's only when we step outside of what we're used to that we realize our need, our hunger, and our smallness (which is why most people don't care to venture out). But this is how we grow. When we let down our self-preserving guard, when we admit our need, and when we acknowledge our hunger, God comes rushing in to meet us.

God knows what will bless us and what will destroy us. He commands our obedience because He has our best interest at heart. He did not offer us all He had only to be listened to occasionally. Nor was the sacrifice of His Son for our sin to be considered one of many options for entrance to heaven. He is the way, the truth, and the life (John 14:6). We can either respond to this priceless gift by trusting His love, entrusting ourselves to Him, and allowing Him to transform us, or we can deny the power of the cross and miss the whole reason He came.

Attempting to live with one foot in the kingdom and one foot in the trappings of this world makes no sense at all. Someone once said the most miserable people on the planet are uncommitted Christians. Ouch. But so understandable. Think about it. When God sent His one and only Son to die for our sins, to pay our debt, and to defeat the devil's hold on us, He did so *to set us free*. No small thing. In fact, Jesus's epic sacrifice and victory blew the doors off the Enemy's claim on us. When we—as professing Christians—live beneath our spiritual privilege, shrug our shoulders at faith, or give a nod to God while living the way we choose, it reveals a total misunderstanding of our nature and of our need. Jesus's gift *to us* requires a sincere and genuine response *from us*. Anything less means we're not really paying attention to the price He paid and the victory He won for us.

He knows how easy it is to follow the crowd, to do what everybody else is doing. He knows it's much harder to do something different. That's why He promised to help us. God's Word cuts through the ever-shifting fads and trends in our culture and gives us a plumb line for how to live.

> God is working in you, giving you the desire and the power to
> do what pleases him (Philippians 2:13).

Notice the love and care in the following verses. Also notice that His promises depend on our obedience:

> The Lord will guarantee a blessing on everything you do and
> will fill your storehouses with grain. The Lord your God will
> bless you in the land he is giving you. If you obey the com-
> mands of the Lord your God and walk in his ways, the Lord
> will establish you as his holy people as he swore he would do
> (Deuteronomy 28:8-9).

As you read the next passage, slow down and think about the times you trusted in your own wisdom. Notice the benefit of walking in the fear of the Lord, turning your back on evil, and giving Him the best of what you have. As uncomfortable as it is to receive correction (from people and the Word of God), consider it something that gives you a holy shove outside your comfort zone and helps you to grow. Notice also the words *fill* and *overflow* in this passage:

> Don't be impressed with your own wisdom. Instead, fear the
> Lord and turn away from evil. Then you will have healing for
> your body and strength for your bones. Honor the Lord with
> your wealth and with the best part of everything you produce.

Then he will fill your barns with grain, and your vats will over-flow with good wine. My child, don't reject the LORD's discipline, and don't be upset when he corrects you. For the LORD corrects those he loves, just as a father corrects a child in whom he delights (Proverbs 3:7-12).

As you empty yourself out to be filled by the only One who can satisfy, you will feel vulnerable. The enemy of your soul will tempt you to be afraid. Jesus understands. Read the following verses and be strengthened by His love for you.

Don't be afraid, for I am with you. Do not be discouraged, for *I am your God. I will strengthen you and help you...* Then you will rejoice in the LORD. You will glory in the Holy One of Israel (Isaiah 41:10,16, emphasis added).

He deserves our trust. He is so faithful and strong. That is why the Enemy works tirelessly to keep us from knowing what we possess in the Lord. Speaking of the Enemy, remember that he comes to steal what's been given to you, kill all that's thriving around you, and destroy your hopes and dreams. Thankfully, God is far more powerful than the enemy of your soul, and He offers to help you do more than just survive; He wants you to thrive.

The thief comes only to steal and kill and destroy; I came that they may have life, and have it abundantly (John 10:10 RSV).

The thief's purpose is to steal and kill and destroy. My purpose is to give them a rich and satisfying life (John 10:10).

He Has More for You

I'm sure you've noticed by now that we're looking at verses that speak of being filled, to be made complete. Even typing them out for you strengthens my own faith. Do you want to be "made complete with all the fullness of life and power that comes from God"? Ask God to bring this next verse to life for you:

> May you experience the love of Christ, though it is too great to understand fully. *Then* you will be made complete with all the fullness of life and power that comes from God (Ephesians 3:19, emphasis added).

To grow spiritually, we need to acquire a taste for the things of God. When we do, we begin to experience an increase in hunger, thirst, and knowledge of the One who makes all things grow, so that we can grow into the fullness of all He created us to be.

> Like newborn babies, *you must crave* pure spiritual milk *so that* you will grow into a full experience of salvation. Cry out for this nourishment, now that you have had a taste of the Lord's kindness (1 Peter 2:2-3, emphasis added).

Ask Him. Ask Him to heal you, fill you, deliver you, and make you whole. If you ask Him, He will do it. His process may be different from what you expect, but there's no mistaking freedom. When you're free and full, you won't wonder about it; *you'll know*. Beloved sister, let Him fill every dark and dreary place, every low and lonely place, every budding hope and dream. Ask Him to work wonders in your life. He will.

Read God's invitation to you. Give Him your full attention. I promise you, there's not a better offer out there.

> Hey there! All who are thirsty, come to the water! Are you penniless? Come anyway—buy and eat! Come, buy your drinks, buy wine and milk. Buy without money—everything's free! Why do you spend your money on junk food, your hard-earned cash on cotton candy? Listen to me, listen well: Eat only the best, fill yourself with only the finest. Pay attention,

come close now, listen carefully to my life-giving, life-nourishing words. I'm making a lasting covenant commitment with you, the same that I made with David: sure, solid, enduring love…Seek GOD while he's here to be found, pray to him while he's close at hand. Let the wicked abandon their way of life and the evil their way of thinking. Let them come back to GOD, who is merciful, come back to our GOD, who is lavish with forgiveness (Isaiah 55:1-3,6-7 MSG).

As we move into the topic of how we nourish our souls, be encouraged to know that no matter where you are with God—whether you've wandered away, stayed close, or never officially met Him—He has more for you. Whatever aspects of His character you've discovered, countless other treasures are yet to be uncovered in your relationship with Him. Remember, the Bible tells us our *fullness* of joy is found in *His* presence (Psalm 16:11 NKJV). *Nothing* satisfies like He does. Every empty place, every hunger, and every hope will find its fullness in the abounding, immeasurable presence of God.

When our boys were young, we had a snack cupboard where we kept raisins, trail mix, snack bars, popcorn, and so on. When you opened the cupboard, you saw a big sign that said, "No Snacks on an Empty Stomach!" My three big teenage boys could easily polish off everything in that cupboard in a matter of minutes. In fact, they've done it plenty of times. Then, when dinnertime rolled around, they had no room for the good stuff. Their bellies were full, but their bodies remained undernourished.

Ecclesiastes 6:7 says, "We work to feed our appetites; meanwhile our souls go hungry" (MSG). When we fill ourselves up on the things of the world, we have a sense of "fullness" while our spiritual lives go unnourished. Our quick fix society allows us access to things so we never have to fully experience certain levels of hunger, pain, desire, or loneliness. We eat, we shop, we drink, we watch, and we numb ourselves, and then we miss out on the deeper life. Obviously, this is not to say that eating food, buying certain items, watching certain movies, or taking certain medicines is bad. It's only bad when those things are used to fill a place meant for God.

When we come to the place where we can honestly admit and face our need, He will honestly meet us there. Honesty sounds something like this:

"The truth is, I feel especially alone in a large crowd. That's why I get loud and draw all kinds of attention to myself."

"The truth is, I am still very angry, and I don't know how not to be, so I drink or I eat."

"The truth is, I cannot let go of my past, so I constantly strive to achieve and prove my worth."

"The truth is, I always feel 'less than,' so I go shopping and buy things that are 'better than.'"

When we quit filling ourselves up on the junk food of this world and allow ourselves to feel the emptiness, the hunger, and the pain in our souls—and then ask God to do something about it—He will meet us, fill us, and more than satisfy our deepest needs.

Father in heaven,

Thank You for loving me. You are long-suffering, patient, and kind. Forgive me for grabbing quick fixes rather than waiting for the best of what You have for me. Lord God, increase my hunger and thirst for You. Help me desire the things that nourish my soul. Grant me the ability to see the bigger picture and to know when I am cutting corners for convenience, which causes me to miss the greater blessing. Give me an eternal perspective so that I might choose life and nourishment every single day. In Your precious name, I pray, amen.

Steps Toward Health

- I will pause, pray, and ask God to search my heart. I will ask

Him to show me what I use to numb my pain, discomfort, boredom, and so on.

- I will lay this thing down for a time (a partial fast) for the purpose of seeking a deeper walk with the Lord.

- I will share this with a godly friend for the sake of accountability.

- I will remember every day, as I wrestle with the temptations and distractions of life, that I am someone God thoroughly enjoys.

- I will continue to pursue a simpler life.

Try This

- *Pause regularly and pray.* "Nourish my soul, Lord. Make me whole. May my life reflect more of You and less of me. Create in me a heart to do Your will, to see from Your perspective, and to serve You above all. Amen."

- *Pursue and protect your devotional times.* Spend regular time with God. Look forward with expectation to increased amounts of time with Him.

- *Every morning proclaim, "I'm alive in Christ!"* Say this out loud and let these words trump every lesser message that comes your way. Look for Him throughout the day. He provides nourishment in many creative ways. Allow Him to nourish you.

- *Pray before you read the Word of God.* Ask for an increased capacity to understand the hidden truths in the Word of God. Ask the Lord to use the Word to speak directly into your life. This will radically change your perspective and priorities.

- *Meet Him in a different place.* Don't allow your devotional life to become rote or commonplace. Keep your love affair alive. Sometimes I lie facedown on the floor and pray, "Oh, Father, if I could get any lower I would; You are so holy; have mercy on this soul of mine." Other times I recline in His presence and just rest in Him. I approach Him as an intimate lover and friend. Often I sit in total silence for extended periods of time and just listen to what He has to say. He is my Counselor, and when I spend more time listening than talking, my soul is nourished. Sometimes when I'm all alone in my house, I twirl and dance to a beautiful song. I celebrate all He has provided, and it makes me want to dance.

- *Place Scripture where you spend a lot of time.* Find a verse that ministers to your heart. Look often at the Scripture, think about it, look out the window, and breathe a prayer to God.

- *Find an accountability partner.* Choose someone you know is serious about following the Lord. Dare to ask the hard questions of each other, like, "More important than how you are feeling, how are you *thinking* lately?" or "How is your devotional life?" or "Are your relationships clean?" Meet regularly. Begin and end your meetings with prayer. This will help keep you on track.

- *Cherish the quiet.* When you come upon a quiet moment, don't fill it with noise. Don't waste a bunch of time on your phone. Don't call a friend every time you have a need. Don't turn on the TV. Refuse to get sucked into the black hole of social media. Just let it be you and God. Tell your soul He's more than enough for you. Then ask Him to show you what your soul truly needs (e.g., rest, healing, nourishment, truth). Occasionally allow those sacred times to become Sabbath moments. Acknowledge Him in the quiet. Whether or not you feel Him, He will nourish you.

- *Lie down and look up.* Once in a while, turn on some praise music, lie down, and picture yourself in the presence of God. Just rest there. I promise it will do something for you.

- *Don't neglect gathering with other believers.* Though these private sacred spaces are essential to a deeper faith walk, we also need one another to grow. Don't give up on church; don't be too quick to skip Bible study; don't give up too quickly on your life-group. Remind your soul, *I need other believers in my life and they need me. Together we'll become all Christ dreamed for us to be.*

Balance Application

God will fill us when we're not filling ourselves with something else. Conversely, when we've already filled our minds and hearts (and stomachs) with the things of this world, we have no more room for Him. To maintain a life of balance, we must stay close to and be nourished by our Source of life. We may last a little while on the world's junk food, but it will ultimately fail us.

Every day we make deposits into our lives. Often we don't see the results of those deposits right away. At first they create "invisible changes." But eventually our inward choices catch up with our outward lives. We have the choice each day to either "just get by" or boldly invest in something much bigger than ourselves. God is everywhere and hugely active on the earth today, but the significance is lost on us if we're too busy and too distracted to notice. Spiritual parallels and connections are in almost anything we do, from gardening to baking, from loving our children to loving our spouse. God's truths and His lessons are woven into the fabric of life. God is speaking and pouring Himself out to a waiting and watching world. The problem is, most people are neither waiting nor watching. Oh, may we feast on the best of what God has for us! There's a world out there in need of the fresh life to which we have access.

Study Time

1. Read Mark 8:1-8. In a few sentences, summarize what happened here. Describe Jesus's heart for the people, describe the need, describe the process of meeting the need, and describe the outcome.

2. Think about that for a moment. People investing their time, risking hunger just to have more of Jesus. Seven loaves, four

thousand plus people. The multitudes ate until they were *full*.
More than enough was left over. How big is our God?

3. Read Mark 8:11. Recall a time when someone approached
   you with the intent to accuse and argue with you. How did
   that feel? Imagine Jesus. He had just ministered to thousands
   of people with great care and compassion. He immediately
   hopped into a boat to go to the next place and was confronted
   by prideful, accusatory religious leaders. Describe how you
   think He felt.

4. Read Mark 8:12. What was Jesus's response to their demands?
   Why do you think He responded this way? Explain.

5. Read Mark 8:13-14. The disciples forgot their food for the day.
   Just a note here: Even when we forget, God is still enough.

6. Read Mark 8:15. Recall again that time when you were verbally
   "assaulted" by someone. As I mentioned earlier in the book,
   it can take your nervous system up to two days to settle down
   from an intense confrontation. Jesus loves His disciples and
   is concerned that, as their ministry grows, they not become
   prideful, demanding, and arrogant. With that in mind, read
   verse 15 again.

7. Read Mark 8:16. Contrast the disciples' concerns and perspective with that of Jesus's.

8. Read Mark 8:17-21. Hear the passion in Jesus's voice. He
   is exasperated that after they witnessed such an incredible
   miracle, their eyes so quickly went back to their appetite and
   immediate need. Think about that in terms of your own
   life. (Take your time. This deserves some thought.) We must
   remember that without faith, it is impossible to please Him
   (Hebrews 11:6).

9. It's as if Jesus is saying, "Concern yourselves not with provision; I own it all. Concern yourselves with the poison of pride.
   Don't strive to satisfy your appetite, be earnest in guarding
   your heart." We often mix up our job and God's job. Despite

the good things God has done for you, do you worry more than trust in any areas of your life? Write them down. Write a prayer asking for forgiveness and more faith.

10. Pause and pray that you will be *filled* with more of God, and that your perspective will reflect a heart of faith.

Personal Reflection

1. This week we're learning about the importance of feasting on and filling up on the things of God so we won't ruin our appetite with what weakens us. What adjustment can you make and what's one habit you can fast from to create more space for the things of God in your life?

2. Consider your default responses when you're uncomfortable, bored, anxious, and so on. Do you scroll through your phone, flip on the TV, search the Internet, or binge watch Netflix? With what do you try to fill the empty places? What's the consistent emotion that compels you to turn to these things? Boredom, stress, fear, anxiety, insecurity, loneliness? Sharon Garlough Brown suggests we should linger with what provokes us because God will meet us there and teach us something about ourselves and about Him.

3. What might Jesus have to say to you about this revelation? Remember, His voice always calls us upward.

This Week's Goal:

_____

_____

_____

God's Promise to Me:

_____

_____

_____

What Keeps You Balanced, Grounded?

Susie, I've learned so much from what you've written, so let me paraphrase some of the things I've learned from you in the past year:

- Stop listening to the "should-dos" and always go back to Jesus's voice of peace.
- Stop comparing. Everyone's life is open to a page of their book; we can see only one page, not the whole story. So stop comparing!
- I'm learning to be content to be misunderstood.
- I'm pondering the "tithe of the time" and what my devotional life might look like as a mom of four littles.
- And for sure, sleep. Even if it means passing up some of my beloved-introvert-craving quiet time at night!

—Sarah

Eleven

A Healthy Spiritual Diet

An intelligent person is always eager to take in more truth; fools feed on fast-food fads and fancies.
PROVERBS 15:14 MSG

Every time I prepare for a speaking engagement, I enter a time of fasting. I fast from certain foods or meals, I fast from media, and I even sometimes fast from my cell phone. I use that extra time for prayer, study of the Word, and extended periods of silence in God's presence. This allows me to focus and prepare my heart, and most of all, to hear from God. Especially during my times of silence I get the clearest sense of what I'm supposed to say at the upcoming engagement.

We're empty nesters now, so my recovery time looks different. But back when we still had kids at home, I was always excited to walk in the door after my event and be welcomed home by my boys and my husband. After I dropped my bags in the entryway, we'd all gather in the living room, and I'd share how God moved in the hearts of the women. I often choked up when I described some of the significant ways women truly encountered God in a way that changed them. We sometimes prayed together and thanked the Lord for what He'd done and what He would continue to do. After this sweet time with my family, I'd unpack my bags and then usually snuggle up with a favorite novel, a bowl of popcorn, and the remote control (so I could see what was going on in the news). When my kids were younger, I didn't have this luxury to enjoy. I was and am thankful for this time of rest and replenishment.

After one event, God moved in such a profound way that it left me speechless, and I heard from a woman who said it took her three days to find the words to share how God touched her during this time. Another woman wrote to me and said she walked into the session with a severe sinus infection and walked out without one. I was not speaking about healing; I was talking about prayer. But the presence of God was so strong in that sanctuary, I could have said nothing and women would have experienced God in a profound way.

When I arrived home after this event, I was still stunned. The thought of curling up with a big bowl of buttered popcorn just didn't seem right. Nothing about my little treats was sinful or excessive, but at that moment they didn't even sound good to me. I was exhausted, but more than that, I was hungry; not physically hungry, but *starving* for more of what I experienced at that event. Clearly, I'd tasted something far beyond me.

I felt compelled to continue my fast for the sake of gaining a deeper understanding of what God had just done. I crawled into bed and pulled the covers up around me. I thanked God for what we'd just experienced. "What was that, Lord? Reveal Your heart to me. I want more of You. Show me more of You."

Curled up in a little ball as I whispered my prayer, I dozed off and had a vivid dream (unusual for me at the time). I saw a deep purplish-blue sky with clouds rumbling and moving. Lightning was shooting through the darkness. This display of God's power hovered just overhead. Below, people walked along chatting, completely unaware of the powerful sight just above them. Occasionally a mother would stop, reach up, grab a handful of the "power," put it on her children, and then go about her business. Some people never looked up; they just walked along, totally caught up in their earthly affairs. Others looked up and took hold of the power only in times of crisis. But once in a while, someone took hold of every ounce she could grab to place it on her kids, her marriage, and her own heart. Even on others as they walked by. It was as though she found the secret to a powerful life and was going to lay hold of everything made available to her. She would not be distracted by the things around her; she had found the Source of power.

I woke up and pondered this unusual dream, and the Lord whispered this stunning insight to my heart: *Most of My children only scratch the surface of what I have made available to them. If they took hold of everything they had access to, they would change the world.* I was so affected by my speaking event and the dream that followed that I have never stopped praying, "Lord God, help me to lay hold of all You've laid hold of for me. I want to fulfill every last thing You created me for!"

Try to imagine the power God has made available to us. Imagine if we traded our addictions and bad habits for soul nourishment that would heal us, give us a holy confidence, and a strong sense of purpose. What if, instead of living lives where we constantly struggle with overindulgence, always feeding our appetites and comforts, we instead looked to God to meet needs only He is meant to fulfill? Wouldn't it be something to become "flow-through accounts" where we continually accessed all that God wants to give *to* us and *through* us? What if we gained such freedom from the snares of this world that our lives were freed up to live powerfully, to be walking, breathing representatives of the Most High God? Can you imagine how we would change the world? Read the following passages and ask God to help you grasp all that's available to you.

> I also pray that you will understand *the incredible greatness of God's power for us who believe him. This is the same mighty power that raised Christ from the dead* and seated him in the place of honor at God's right hand in the heavenly realms (Ephesians 1:19-20, emphasis added).

Imagine if we traded our addictions and bad habits for soul nourishment that would heal us, give us a holy confidence, and a strong sense of purpose.

I pray that from his glorious, unlimited resources he will empower
you with inner strength through his Spirit... Now all glory to
God, who is able, through his mighty power at work within
us*, to accomplish infinitely more than we might ask or think*
(Ephesians 3:16,20, emphasis added).

What does this have to do with having a healthy spiritual diet?
Everything. Most people eat healthy food because it's good for them.
Over time they acquire a taste for the good stuff and prefer healthy,
nutritious food over junk food. But initially people get on a health kick
because they want change, and to get a different result, they need to
make some different choices. Some want to carry around less weight,
while others just want to feel better. Some want more energy, while
others want to reduce their risk of disease. Some may want to maintain a youthful appearance. Once a person begins to reap the benefits
of a healthy lifestyle, they tend to prefer self-discipline to the path of
least resistance.

As we look at various ways to nourish your soul, remember the lever
principle. Every one of us has a certain level of "input" in our lives,
both physically and spiritually. What changes from season to season
is the degree we take in, meaning there will be seasons when you can
take in more, and seasons when you're forced to live on less. As long as
the other levers (output and rest) also adjust at the same time, you will
be able to maintain a certain sense of balance wherever life finds you.

That said, we must also remember that God's supply is never short.
Whether we're in a season chasing little ones, raising school-age kids,
or sitting at the bedside of a loved one who is ill, God *will* supply *all*
our needs. Our part is to seize every moment we can throughout the
day to acknowledge God, ask for His help and direction, and then listen for His voice. One of my favorite verses is Psalm 116:9. "I walk in
the Lord's presence as I live here on earth!" If we approach every day
with the mind-set that God is with us and longs for us to draw on His
strength, we will find strength for the task, wisdom for direction, and
love that fills every gap.

Precious sister, draw near to Him. He has untapped storehouses of provision for you—more than you could ever use. And He Himself is the best gift of all, and you already have Him.

Nourishment for My Spiritual Body

How wonderful it is to have a heavenly Father who is endless in His love for us and boundless in His supply on our behalf. When we plumb the depths of the power of God in our lives, nothing else compares. His mercies are new every morning, and His faithfulness is beyond our comprehension (Lamentations 3:22-23 NKJV). We have access to all of God's riches, which leaves us without a reason for living a stale and stagnant life. Jesus said to His disciples, "I have a kind of food you know nothing about" (John 4:32), and again He said, "My nourishment comes from doing the will of God, who sent me, and from finishing his work" (John 4:34).

Since Jesus is our Source, it is important to remember what our spiritual food is for.

Spiritual food is for drowning our sorrows. "Surely He took up our pain and bore our suffering" (Isaiah 53:4 NIV). As we feed on the Word of God and spend time in His presence, He will heal us, deliver us, and get us back on our feet again. You may be going through grief or a time of loss, and the Word of God is full of verses that will identify with your pain and comfort you in your sorrow. The Bible is also filled with hope, and as you think on the verses that mean something to you, you will find your soul restored.

Spiritual food is an outlet for our anger. "But you, LORD, are a compassionate and gracious God, slow to anger, abounding in love and faithfulness" (Psalm 86:15 NIV). People will hurt and betray you. They will treat you unkindly, and if you are human, this will make you mad. But when you take your anger to the Lord, when you humble yourself before Him and confess your own sin, He becomes your greatest defender. When you submit yourself to Him, He will help you to let go of the anger and gain victory over your situation.

Spiritual food is an outlet for boredom. "You light a lamp for me. The

LORD, my God, lights up my darkness" (Psalm 18:28). Often we're bored because we've lost our sense of gratitude and wonder. The Bible says God inhabits the praises of His people (Psalm 22:3 KJV). Try this once. Take a few moments and start thanking the Lord for everything you can think of... *Thank You, Lord, for running water and for a roof over my head. Thank You, Lord, for the laughter of my children. Thank You, Lord, for my eyesight*...If you take a moment to enter the presence of the living God, your perspective will change and your soul will be nourished beyond belief.

Spiritual food is not meant only to fuel us, but for our enjoyment too. "The LORD is my shepherd; I have all that I need. He lets me rest in green meadows; he leads me beside peaceful streams. He renews my strength. He guides me along right paths, bringing honor to his name" (Psalm 23:1-3). Just as we acquire a taste for certain foods, we acquire a hunger for the presence of the Lord as we spend more and more time with Him. If you struggle with even having a desire to nourish yourself spiritually, start there. Be honest and pray, "Lord, I have no desire to draw near. Please make me hunger for Your Word and Your Presence. Help me know You are all I need. Amen."

Spiritual Food Laws to Live By

Keep it colorful. Don't overload on only one choice of nourishment (for example, one speaker, one author, one musician). Jesus has equipped a multitude of His children for the building up of His kingdom. When you feast on the fruit of only one of His servants, you run the risk of becoming narrow in your thinking and acceptance of how things should be communicated. Remember this: *The narrow road and a narrow mind are not the same thing.* God speaks in many ways, even through donkeys (Numbers 22:21-33), and it is His great pleasure to do so. Be open to all He is saying and doing around you. Listen to your children; He often speaks through them. When you humble yourself and acquire a taste for the different reflections of Christ's character, you will be more well-rounded.

A secret isn't a secret. Walk in the light where there is fellowship, freedom, and peace. Be real about your struggles. If you can't go to church to get free, where can you? Challenges feel much weightier when we hide our secrets in fear, and the Enemy wants it that way. The truth is you are not alone, you are not the first to struggle in this area, and nothing is worth hiding when it keeps us from the freedom we were made for. The enemy of your soul will try to convince you that keeping your struggles in the dark will keep you from being exposed, but *he's* the one who doesn't want to be exposed for the liar he is.

Jesus died for your sins. When you bring your struggles into the light, you can see them for what they are. When you take them to the cross, Jesus will set you free. "When I refused to confess my sin, my body wasted away, and I groaned all day long" (Psalm 32:3). "Yes, what joy for those whose record the LORD has cleared of guilt, whose lives are lived in complete honesty!" (Psalm 32:2). For further study, read 1 John 1:7-9.

Look past it. One day I was preoccupied by several things. I caught myself staring out the window as I mulled my worries over in my mind. Well, I wasn't staring out the window; I was staring *at* the window. A dirty spot on the window caught my gaze. My eyes landed on that spot while my mind ran wild with things I had no control over. Out of the corner of my eye I saw movement. I snapped out of my daydream to see a jogger going by. Then I looked up and saw the trees blowing in the breeze. A red cardinal landed on a nearby branch.

It was a lovely day and a perfect lesson. How often do we fix our minds and our focus on our worries and miss the bigger picture? Yes, we need to acknowledge our problems, but we should not fixate on them. Scripture tells us to keep our eyes on Jesus (Hebrews 12:2). Every day, more often than not, acknowledge your need, take it to God, and then look past your circumstances to the handiwork of God. Remind yourself that if He can create a world in six days, He can solve your problems without much effort.

Remember the metabolic rule. If we go too long without "eating," our spiritual metabolism will slow down and we will begin to lose our taste for the things of God. Going too long without nourishing our souls will cause a decline in our spiritual energy. Once we've surrendered to Christ, we are a new creation. But if we pay little attention to nourishing our souls, we affect our fellowship with Him. If our fellowship with Jesus is weak, we will be weak, and we'll have little strength to stand when the storms hit. Take moments throughout the day to notice the sky and breathe a prayer. Buy a flip calendar with Scripture verses and quotations and look at it regularly throughout the day. Carry a small book in your purse—one that makes you think and challenges your faith—and open it when you're in a waiting room, in a grocery line, and so on. Feed your soul regularly throughout the day.

Do "eat" at night. Though it's best not to eat food at night, it's wonderful to end your day with a little soul nourishment. Keep a devotional at your bedside and close the day with thoughts of grace to cover your mistakes, with faith that God will protect everything you love, and with hope for a fruitful day tomorrow. The Bible says it is good to praise the Lord, to proclaim His love in the morning and His faithfulness at night (Psalm 92:2).

Practice partial fasts. I covered this in the first section of this book, but I want to address it again on a slightly deeper level. Whenever you decide to take a break from something you've allowed to become a habit in your life, it will be difficult at first. Just as fasting from food starts a detoxification process that, among other things, is revealed on the tongue, fasting from things we have an unhealthy attachment to also brings things to the surface of the tongue. You may become edgy, you may say things you don't mean, and you may even become angry. As soon as some people encounter these unpleasant "symptoms," they return to their *thing* and the symptoms go away. But a response is all the more reason to press through and claim victory over what has a hold on you.

Do you want to know true soul freedom? Refuse to accommodate your own captivity. When you've developed a habit that weakens or distracts you, decide immediately to say no to yourself and make yourself deal with it. Jesus wants to fill that space with life, peace, and an abundance you'll love. And He will help you.

Listen. Really listen. When you approach each day with your ears wide open, full of expectancy that God wants to speak to you, you will be nourished beyond your expectations. Next time you hear a worship song on the radio, focus your attention on the words and ponder how they apply to you. Listen to your children. Next time they have something to say to you, stop what you're doing, get low, and look them right in the eye. Take in all their features and delight in the way God designed them. Hear their words and be blessed by their presence in your life. When a friend compliments you, let it in. Allow yourself to be nourished by her words. Next time you're in church, listen closely to the sermon. Ask the Lord to show you what your response should be to the message you've just heard. Listen to the birds sing. Listen to laughter. Be selective about what you listen to.

Guard your heart. Keep your heart a sacred place—don't let weeds of bitterness and discontentment sprout up. This requires a diligent defense (Proverbs 4:23) and an intentional pursuit of purity. As soon as you notice yourself picking up an offense against someone or something, get down on your knees and relinquish your rights to the Lord. God will at times allow hurtful and unjust things to happen to us. Through many of these trials I learned that God was at work, purifying my heart, renewing my mind, and strengthening my resolve to love. This is no small task. Purity, humility, and love are not flowery, gooey emotions. They are traits wrought through the thickest of battles and the fiercest of fights. No one just happens upon a heart free of malice and hardness. Love and guard your heart, and keep it a sweet and fresh place.

Take responsibility for your spiritual health. It is not your pastor's job or your husband's job or your friend's job to make sure you stay on track. Granted, the Lord wants us to surround ourselves with people who can be of benefit to our spiritual health, but you are the one who will decide what attitudes you will embrace, what thoughts you will entertain, and where you will spend your time. You will stand before God and give account for the return He receives on His investment in you.

Ask the Lord to reveal to you where you are weak. This is good for you to know, because you can bet that the enemy of your soul knows not only your weaknesses, but how you can be tempted. This is why, as uncomfortable as it is, we must honestly face our spiritual deficiencies so our walls can be fortified and we can stand strong when the elements rage.[1] Don't look for excuses for your weakness. Look instead for ways to be strengthened.

Use your strength. When you feel strong in the Lord, use that strength to take extra ground. In other words, pray with more passion, serve with more presence, and listen with more diligence. If God has given you a special time of favor, it isn't just for your health. It's because He has something more for you to do and He trusts you to do it. If you feel weak and fragile, hang on to this verse: "A bruised reed he will not break, and a dimly burning wick he will not quench; he will faithfully bring forth justice" (Isaiah 42:3 RSV). Picture Him cupping His hands around you as the elements rage. Imagine Him protecting you while the wind blows. He will breathe new life and strength into you. Take Him at His word. When you are weak, hang on. When you are strong, take extra ground.

Join a Bible study. Many wonderful Bible studies are available. Powerful things happen when women come together for fellowship and spiritual growth. Whether or not you believe it, you have much to offer other women, and they have much to offer you. We really need one another. You might be surprised to find that when you show up on those days when it would have been easier to stay home, God will especially use you, speak to you, or bless you in some special way.

Carve out your quiet time. As I mentioned earlier, years ago when my sons were little, I was fighting a terrible disease at the same time. My boys were close in age, and combining their endless energy with my fatigue and sickness, life was anything but settled and peaceful. I came into my marriage accustomed to regular quiet times, and yet my life drastically changed almost overnight. I went to the Lord *regularly* and passionately appealed to Him, "You are capable of moving heaven and earth for Your children. I want time with You. You want time with me. Your Word promises that when I ask for something in accordance with Your will, I can be sure I'll receive it. I will spend my pitiful ten minutes doing devotions since that's all the quiet time available for me right now. I will show up for my quiet times and consider them a 'tithe of the time.' I trust that as I give You my few minutes, You'll see me as You did the boy on the hillside who gave You his lunch. You multiplied his gift beyond belief! I trust You to multiply my devotional time beyond belief. I want to walk closely with You—You want this for me too. I will watch and see what You will do."

A miraculous thing happened; the boys began playing together for longer periods of time without incident. Now, I will confess, I did sort of tell them that unless the house was on fire they needed to play nicely until I was done praying, but they got used to the priority of my prayer time. Over time, despite my having three little, active boys, the Lord provided ample amounts of study and prayer time. He became my strength through the darkest of valleys. Give Him what little time you have. Ask Him to give you more, and expect that He will. He loves prayers like that because He loves to spend time with you.

A. W. Tozer wrote this regarding your time with the Lord:

Retire from the world each day to some private spot, even if it be only the bedroom (for a while I retreated to the furnace room for want of a better place). Stay in the secret place till the surrounding noises begin to fade out of your heart and a sense of God's presence envelops you. Deliberately tune out the unpleasant sounds and come out of your closet determined not to hear them. Listen for the inward voice till you learn to recognize it. Stop trying to compete with others. Give yourself to God and then be what and who you are without regard to what others think. Reduce your interests to a few. Don't try to know what will be of no service to you...Pray for a single eye. Read less, but read more of what is important to your inner life. Never let your mind remain scattered for very long. Call home your roving thoughts. Gaze on Christ with the eyes of your soul. Practice spiritual concentration.[2]

God in heaven,

I long to have more of You. Take me to that higher place, Lord. Keep me from swallowing the world's lies when You've prepared for me a feast of healing truths. Help me to take You at Your word. Increase my capacity to know You. Increase my desire to spend time in Your presence. More than anything, help me grasp Your love for me, for that will affect everything I think and do. I hunger for You, Lord. Make me hunger more. Amen.

Steps Toward Health

- I will take an honest look at my spiritual diet. I will consider it a priority to take the steps needed to nourish myself spiritually.

- I will not feel guilty or consider it a waste of time to sit down to pray or to just be quiet before the Lord. I will think of these times as an investment and know that God will bring a great return in my life and the lives around me as a result.

- I will ask God which of the Spiritual Food Laws I need to apply in my life.

- I will refuse to look at this information as yet another impossible list of tasks I must accomplish; rather, I will pick and choose what will help me to be spiritually healthy.

- I will ask God to show me where I waste the most time. (Remember, in Christ, there's *no* condemnation. When we take inventory of our growth areas, it is always about invitation, so we can apprehend the best of what God has for us.)

- I will ask God to increase my hunger for Him.

Try This

- Purchase Mary Tileston's book *Joy and Strength* or L.B. Cowman's book *Streams in the Desert*. These inexpensive little devotionals are packed with words from giants of the faith. If you want a colorful spiritual diet, nourish yourself on the wisdom of those who have gone before us.

- Rent the movie *The Hiding Place*. Allow this film to speak to you on many levels. Be thankful for the freedom and provisions you enjoy. Be inspired by the tenacity of this family's faith. Notice how Corrie and her sister adjust to their wretched circumstances. They found a place of fruitfulness in the darkness of a prison camp. Amid their struggle, they were nourished by God's Word, and they gave it away.

- Dare to ask God this question: Lord, what do I have in my hand that You want, so that I can take hold of more of You?

- Spend less time indulging yourself this week and more time nourishing yourself.

- Buy a notebook or a journal and begin to record what God is saying to you (this will nourish you now *and* later when you look back on it).

- Make it your practice to keep your ears and eyes wide open all day long. Be aware of all that God is doing around you. Obey Him when He tells you to do something.

Balance Application

The heavens are bursting with blessing, provision, and promise. God waits for us and longs to bless us. Every time we look up and call on Him to influence our lives, He will. Every time we go without something for the purpose of seeking Him more, we will receive far more than we gave up. When we embrace every sacred moment that comes our way as a chance to love God more, listen to His voice, and do what He says, our lives become living, breathing examples of Christ's continued work on earth. To be nourished by the Most High God is our greatest privilege. It's what gives us the strength to do things far beyond us.

Study Time

1. Read Hebrews 12:1.
2. What are the weights in your life that slow you down?
3. What do you get tangled up in?
4. If Jesus sat down next to you, what do you think He would tell you about these weights? What will you do about them?
5. Read Luke 12:22-30. Read it again.
6. Share or write how this passage applies to you.
7. Look at Luke 12:31.
8. What is the promise? What's the contingency?
9. Do you need to make changes in your life so you can better nourish yourself (so you'll be better strengthened for kingdom work)?
10. Write down a prayer asking God to help you do what He is calling you to do.

Personal Reflection

1. This week we're learning about the power of cultivating a taste for the presence of God. When was the last time you enjoyed time just resting in His presence and listening for what He has to say? How did that experience make an impact on you? Really dig deep on this one and give more than a surface answer.
2. Consider the fact that when you come into God's presence, He invites you to come with holy confidence (Ephesians 3:12). Why do you suppose He loves spending time with you?

3. What spiritual practice makes you think more about the things of eternity than the things of earth (e.g., journaling, prayer, worship, reading Scripture, gathering with other believers)? How might you make more space in your life for this spiritual practice?

This Week's Goal:

_____

_____

_____

God's Promise to Me:

_____

_____

_____

What Keeps You Balanced, Grounded?

I get out of balance when I'm out of the Word. Also, I need physical rest. If I try to pack too much in my schedule, I get sick (and crabby). So I stay grounded when I stay in the Word. And when I refuse to get over-busy.

—Heidi

Twelve

A Healthy Thought Life

Fix your thoughts on what is true. and honorable, and right, and pure, and lovely, and admirable. Think about things that are excellent and worthy of praise.

<small>PHILIPPIANS 4:8</small>

When I was young, several teenage boys from our neighborhood pinned my ankles and my wrists to the ground, and put their hands all over me. One day I was a naïve, innocent girl; the next day I was fearful, anxious, and all too aware of my "nakedness." For the rest of my teen years and most of my young adult life, I tried to crawl out of my black hole of insecurity. I leaned heavily upon my athletic ability in the hopes that my achievements would balance the scales in my mind. I didn't want the "lost cause" side to win. Unfortunately, covering lies with achievements does not turn lies into truths.

Though I had a lot of passion as a Christ-follower, I lacked real freedom and peace. Though I consistently spent time with the Lord, read the Bible, and memorized Scripture, I couldn't hang on to the joy God had promised me. One day while watching an old cartoon with my kids, I got a clear picture of myself. (It was quite a few years ago so I can't remember the cartoon. I think it was Bugs Bunny.) One of the characters took several arrows to the gut. He pulled them out and went about his day. Later on he drank a glass of milk, and guess what happened.

He leaked! That was me! I deposited all these wonderful truths and wisdom into my life, but—due to my perpetual thoughts of fear, worry, and insecurity—much of my soul nourishment leaked right out of me. My inconsistent thought life kept me from "keeping" all God was making available to me. First John 2:24 says, "See that what you have heard from the beginning remains in you" (NIV).

Guard Your Thought Life

Sometimes I embraced the truth. Other times I mulled over my mistakes. I found that if I spent too much time on the mistakes, the devil tacked onto my train of thought a caboose filled with condemnation, accusation, and insecurity.

Did you know that insecurity is just another form of selfishness? When our thoughts are wrapped up in all that is wrong with us or all that we lack, we miss what's beautiful around us and in us. When we are insecure (or prideful, for that matter), we make decisions with "ourselves" in mind.

Our youngest son, Jordan, is now a grown man. When he was young he was terribly shy, sweet, and somewhat insecure. My husband and I prayed for him and constantly told him, "Jordan, you are so important to God and to us. If you're shy in the sense that you have less to say, that's okay. But if you're timid because you're afraid of what people think of you, well, son, that's not okay. You have the God of the universe living inside you, and He commands you not to fear the opinions of others. If you walk in the fear of the Lord, meaning that you respect Him enough to do what He says, you need fear nothing else. God has put too much into you. Don't shrink back because of what others might think."

Those words sunk in over time, and he is now a totally transformed young man. The strengths he possesses were once his weaknesses. Jordan is strong, confident, and funny. He absolutely does not care what people think of him, and yet he remains kind and considerate of others. What power there is in a life that's free of self.

The Bible tells us the pure in heart will see God. When our hearts and minds are pure, we are more able to see what God is doing in our own lives, as well as in the lives of others. If our thoughts are marred by insecurity, anger, or obsessive self-awareness, we miss much of what God is doing, and our choices will drive us further and further away from what will truly fill us.

In her wonderful book *Something More*, Catherine Marshall wrote about a term often used during World War II. The term "beachhead" described a battle that usually took place on the shore. Whoever won the beach often won the bigger battle. Catherine Marshall compares this idea to our thought life. She writes,

> Just so—my life, my body, my affairs are as an island empire that the unholy spirit hopes to win en route to his ultimate objective of my eternal soul. To do that, he too must first gain a beachhead in my life. With that toehold, then he can take his time about gaining control of the rest of me and my affairs— yard by yard, decision by decision.[1]

Look again at the Scripture at the beginning of this chapter and you will find God's standard for a healthy thought life. In that Scripture are eight gatekeepers for guarding your mind. When we intentionally set a watch on our thoughts and refuse entrance to any thought that is beneath God's standard for us, we will literally be transformed. In our pursuit of a higher calling and a healthier life, here lies a nugget of truth we must never let go of: *When we don't allow our thoughts to run wild, they will run deeper.*

Eight Ways to Keep Your Thought Life Safe

Philippians 4:8 says to "fix your thoughts." Stop there. Amid the whirlwind of life, how does one "fix thoughts" on *anything*? The best example I can think of is in this little story I once heard. A man took his young son on a fishing trip. They were in the middle of nowhere when the son desperately needed a bathroom, and the woods wouldn't suffice, if you know what I mean. The only available place was a dive of a bar. It looked pretty run-down, and it was the last place you would want to take your child.

But in they went, father and son, into the smoky, dingy bar. Once they got into the bathroom, the father noticed there were no doors on the stalls. And even worse than that, foul words were written all over the walls of the stalls. The boy sat down on the stool and the father knelt right in front of him. He placed his strong hands on either side of his son's face, got close to him, and said, "Just keep looking at me, son. Just keep looking at me." The boy replied, "Okay, Daddy."

That's what "fixing your eyes" looks like. No matter what foul messages or less than pleasant circumstances surround you, place your precious face in the hands of your Savior and listen to Him. Below are eight ways you can cultivate a healthy thought life, which will truly transform your life.

Gatekeeper 1—Fix your thoughts on what is true. "God's way is perfect. All the LORD's promises prove true. He is a shield for all who look to him for protection" (Psalm 18:30). "For the word of the LORD holds true, and we can trust everything he does" (Psalm 33:4). There's a big difference between what *feels* true and what *is* true. What *feels* true often relates to our value, our situation, or how others see us. We *must* build our thought lives on something far more stable than circumstance. What doesn't change is God's love for you. He is *for* you, not against you. What's also wonderfully true is that every seemingly hopeless situation is a perfect opportunity for God to show you His glory. What's true is that He loves "impossible" situations, because with God all things are possible (Matthew 19:26). A healthy thought life focuses on the truth.

Gatekeeper 2—Fix your thoughts on what is honorable. "Never pay back evil with more evil. Do things in such a way that everyone can see you are honorable" (Romans 12:17). "Be careful to live properly among your unbelieving neighbors. Then even if they accuse you of doing wrong, they will see your honorable behavior, and they will give honor to God when he judges the world" (1 Peter 2:12). I once spent a week praying about this gatekeeper. I asked God to show me what it means to have an honorable thought life. Wow, did He show me! Throughout my week, people pulled out in front of me on the road, snapped at me on the phone, and one (not naming names) threw all his clothes on the floor just two feet shy of the laundry basket.

I asked him, "You can estimate the cost of multimillion dollar buildings down to the last screw, but you repeatedly miss the laundry basket by two feet?" Well, that wasn't such an honorable thought, and worse yet, I spoke it while I was thinking it! (We'll address the short connection between the mind and the mouth in a few chapters.)

My point is that I was provided countless opportunities to forgive, excuse, pray for, and bless others. It's much more fun to bless a friend with a bouquet of flowers than it is to bless a rude stranger with your smiles, your time, and your prayers. But this is where our walk of faith matters most. This is a call to see others and treat them with God's heart in mind. Give some thought to the attribute of honor. Imagine if the world could hear your thoughts all day, every day. A healthy thought life is full of honorable thoughts.

Gatekeeper 3—Fix your thoughts on what is right. "God is my shield, saving those whose hearts are true and right" (Psalm 7:10). "Who may worship in your sanctuary, LORD? Who may enter your presence on your holy hill? Those who lead blameless lives and do what is right, speaking the truth from sincere hearts" (Psalm 15:1-2). God continually invites us to deeper places with Him, but with the invitation comes a charge to do what is right.

Notice that the call is not to fix your thoughts on *your rights*, but rather on what is right before God. It's logical to dislike selfish neighbors, but as God's child it is *right* to be kind to them and pray for them. It makes sense to want to indulge yourself when you are angry, but it is *right* not to rest until you've brought your anger before the Lord. As we humble ourselves and live rightly before God, we will have the defense of heaven on our side; we will have more than we need. It's only when we grasp for ourselves, demanding our rights, that God takes His hands off the situation and allows us to fend for ourselves.

Consider Jesus, the One we follow. He did not consider equality with God a thing to be grasped, but laid His life down because of love (Philippians 2:5-7). Jesus had rights, but He laid them down so *we* could be right with God. As earthbound souls, we become consumed with our own rights and our own ways. A healthy thought life compels us to look up, to concentrate on what is right according to God's Word, and to surrender our agenda because we believe God's ways are higher and greater than our own.

Gatekeeper 4—Fix your thoughts on what is pure. "God blesses those whose hearts are pure, for they will see God" (Matthew 5:8). "Your eye is like a lamp that provides light for your body. When your eye is healthy, your whole body is filled with light. But when it is unhealthy, your body is filled with darkness" (Luke 11:34). Even those who love us most occasionally breathe a heavy sigh because of something we say or do. And yet God, whose standard is far beyond ours, always has a pure heart toward us. So instead of trying *really hard* to have a pure heart, fix your gaze on the One who is pure and true. Let your thoughts be captivated by the purity of His love. When you do this, something happens over time. When your gaze is fixed on heaven and not on what's wrong on earth, your heart becomes purified, and suddenly you become a fresh spring of hope for those who are still living earthbound lives. What you look for, you will find.

Think about this next verse: "Everything is pure to those whose hearts are pure. But nothing is pure to those who are corrupt and unbelieving, because their minds and consciences are corrupted" (Titus 1:15). We were born for another world. We are on a journey to that promised land. We are here for a purpose, and we've been given clear directives. We are not to get tangled up with the messes of dishonesty, deceit, distraction, and destruction. A healthy thought life pursues purity. When we fix our eyes on Jesus, when we keep our hearts and minds pure just as He is pure, we will see more of God. Imagine. What an amazing promise!

Gatekeeper 5—Fix your thoughts on what is lovely. "How lovely is your dwelling place, O LORD of Heaven's Armies" (Psalm 84:1). "Hallelujah! How good it is to sing to our God, for praise is pleasant and lovely" (Psalm 147:1 HCSB). What is lovely? He is! Every time you catch your mind wandering, capture your thoughts and focus them on the One who loves you. Allow your mind to think about the different ways He has shown up in your life and changed it for the better.

Whenever I feel depleted or distracted, I look out the window. Something about trees and the beautiful sky reminds me of God's majesty and beauty. One Thanksgiving holiday, I went back into the woods by our house and placed ten different signs on ten different trees and gold foil-wrapped chocolate coins at the base of each tree. The signs said things like, "Pause and remember the times the Lord rescued you from a difficult situation," "Pause and remember the people God has given you to love," "Pause and remember the ways God has provided for you."

Then we silently led about four family members at a time out to the woods. We gave them a small sack and explained the journey they were about to take. Each time they came to a tree, they were supposed to get low, pause, and remember God's faithfulness by thanking Him for each instance they could recall. Then to symbolize each act of remembrance, they were to place a gold coin in their sack.

What a treasured sacred time this was! Different family members took their time in the woods, and several of them emerged with tearstained cheeks. When dinnertime arrived, we gathered around the table and emptied our sacks of gold coins. The whole table shimmered with gold-foil chocolates—each representing some specific way God had come through for us. As we joined hands and prayed for our meal, Thanksgiving took on a whole new meaning that year. What's lovely to us is God. What's lovely to Him is a thankful heart. A healthy thought life is grateful for the lovely things God provides.

Gatekeeper 6—Fix your eyes on what is admirable. "To the faithful you show yourself faithful; to those with integrity you show integrity" (2 Samuel 22:26). "I know, my God, that you examine our hearts and rejoice when you find integrity there" (1 Chronicles 29:17). How wonderful to imagine God rejoicing when He looks in on our thought life! Imagine Him leaning over and whispering in an angel's ear, "You know, in light of what she's going through, her thoughts are sure admirable. I'm so proud of her." If for no other reason than to bring pleasure to God, it's worth it to think thoughts filled with security, integrity, dignity, and strength. And yet when we do this, we do more than bring God pleasure. We affect and improve our own lives. When we embrace thoughts that are admirable, we begin to make choices that follow suit. Admirable thoughts bring blessing to both heaven and earth. A healthy thought life desires that which is admirable.

Gatekeeper 7—Fix your thoughts on what is excellent. "Think about the things of heaven, not the things of earth" (Colossians 3:2). "Don't envy sinners, but always continue to fear the LORD. You will be rewarded for this; your hope will not be disappointed" (Proverbs 23:17-18). "Excellent" speaks of something high above the norm. Excellent thoughts "look up" more often than they look down. Jesus said in Luke 12:34, "Wherever your treasure is, there the desires of your heart will also be." The glitzy and glamorous things of this world are just trinkets and toys compared to the unfathomable riches of God's grace and love. He never does anything halfway, and He truly has set His affections on us. When we embrace the wonder of who He is and how He is, it'll become almost instinctive for us to think excellent thoughts. And we need a healthy thought life for the trying circumstances of life, like when someone else gets a breakthrough while we're still waiting for ours. It's possible to navigate such times with grace and class, but it's impossible without a heart set on Jesus.

When we see the value of a redeemed thought life, we'll be more earnest in protecting ourselves from toxic thoughts. And we'll be able to look past the clouds on a rainy day, knowing the blue sky is still very much in place. As we lift our gaze, our hopes, and our dreams to the author and finisher of our faith, our minds will fill with excellent thoughts.

Less-than-excellent thoughts get by our gate when our eyes look to the right and left. In other words, our thoughts go rogue when we start to notice what's not happening for us, or what is happening for someone else, or when we feel slighted and nobody apologizes, or when we give a lot of ourselves away and don't get any credit and nobody thanks us. When we look to the right and to the left, we run the risk of opening the gate to many destructive thoughts.

The remedy? We need to be honest with ourselves, acknowledge where our thoughts have wandered, and then quickly return our gaze to the One who won't let us down. When it's all said and done, we'll love our story most, because in Christ's wisdom, it fits us best. Proverbs 17:24 says, "Sensible people keep their eyes glued on wisdom, but a fool's eyes wander to the ends of the earth." A healthy thought life is full of excellent thoughts that rise above our circumstances and hope beyond what our eyes can see.

Gatekeeper 8—Fix your thoughts on what is worthy of praise. "The heavens proclaim the glory of God. The skies display his craftsmanship. Day after day they continue to speak; night after night they make him known. They speak without a sound or word; their voice is never heard; yet their message has gone throughout the earth, and their words to all the world. God has made a home in the heavens for the sun. It bursts forth like a radiant bridegroom after his wedding. It rejoices like a great athlete eager to run the race" (Psalm 19:1-5). Do you see a theme here? God's ways and His work are far above and beyond any earthly thing. As we take our thoughts captive and make them obedient to Christ (2 Corinthians 10:5 NIV), and as we expose and remove the lies from our thought life and replace them with divine truths, *we will be transformed beyond our wildest dreams* (Romans 12:2). When we guard against ingratitude by humbly remaining thankful, and when we keep our thoughts on what is right and true even if it doesn't *feel* true, we keep from *leaking* all that God has poured into us. When we make it a habit to thank Him all day long for every blessing we enjoy, God draws near and the Enemy doesn't dare come near us (because God is right amid His praising people). If you guard your thoughts and keep them in the high place of praise, your thought life will be healthy and secure.

Precious Lord,

Transform my life by renewing the way I think. Oh, how I want to be victorious in this area! One by one, show me, Lord, what lies I have believed, where I have allowed my thoughts to wander, and where I have missed what You have for me. Raise up a new standard in my thought life so that You and the angels will have something wonderful to talk about. I want my life to honor You and bring You pleasure. Be glorified in me. Amen.

Steps Toward Health

- I will spend time with the Lord and listen to what He has to tell me about my thought life.
- I will write down the areas of my thought life God wants to redeem. I will tuck this list in my Bible and pray regularly until I am bearing fruit in my areas of weakness.
- I will acknowledge that though hard things happen in life, nothing happens in my heart and mind without my permission. I will confess my need for God to help me guard my thoughts.
- I will avoid the sin of comparison and statements like "I'll be okay when…" Instead, I'll embrace God's call and timing in my life. I will proclaim that He is faithful.
- I will ask the Lord to continually motivate me and remind me to renew my mind each new day.
- I will think on and speak God's promises out loud, even when they don't feel true, because I'm committed to owning these truths for myself.

Try This

- During times of fatigue, abandon all introspection and just rest. Protect yourself. This is when you are most vulnerable.

- Do *not* give your thoughts free rein during oversensitive moments. If you must, take sides against yourself. Take your thoughts captive and make them obedient to God's truths.

- Never, ever entertain thoughts of what others might think of you. You'll gain nothing from this process; in fact, you'll lose precious time, perspective, and energy—all things you need for a healthy spiritual life. Good or bad, right or wrong, the people whose opinions matter too much to you don't have all the information. Only God does, and He loves you. Proverbs 29:25 says, "Fearing people is a dangerous trap, but trusting the LORD means safety." Do you want to feel safe with people? Fear God. Don't worry about others' gossip; just make sure you don't gossip. Walk in the humble fear of the Lord, and He'll take care of everything else.

- Don't think about yourself for too long. C.S. Lewis called this "diseased introspection." I once pondered this thought and was shocked! I couldn't believe how often I thought about myself. Then I thought more about myself because I couldn't believe how bad I was. Do you see where this could lead? It never pays to dwell on your shortcomings, your deficits, or your downfalls. Acknowledge your need, remember your righteousness and right standing in Christ (*because* of Christ) and look to Him. Let Jesus bring conviction and be teachable when He does. But refuse condemnation or repetitive thoughts on how flawed you are.

- Be thankful. In your thoughts, in your prayers, out loud, and in a song, thank Him every step of the way. This will honor God and nourish your soul.

- Memorize Scripture. The Word is your weapon against the lies of the Enemy, but you must know the truth before you can refute the lies.

- Keep a tight rein on your thoughts. "If then you were raised with Christ, *seek those things which are above,* where Christ is, sitting at the right hand of God. *Set your minds on the things above*, not on things on the earth" (Colossians 3:1-2 NKJV, emphasis added). Ask for God's help, and start putting strict boundaries on your thought life. Do not let your mind go toward anything beneath faith, hope, and love. Ask for a heightened conviction in this area, and as soon as you catch yourself thinking negative thoughts, turn those thoughts into prayers that declare God's faithfulness. As you make this a practice, you'll be surprised to see even your spontaneous responses become healthier and more godly.

Balance Application

I can spend hours studying the Word of God, I can listen to countless sermons, and I can sing every day at the top of my lungs, "God is for me!" But if I don't guard my thoughts, I won't keep my joy and peace. Throughout this book, perhaps you've noticed this underlying theme: Our lives adapt to consistent messages.

When we hear something over and over, be it positive or negative, eventually it sticks with us. As we pursue a healthy thought life, we must give ourselves the gift of consistency. This may take great effort at first, but once we've blazed a new trail in our thought patterns, it will be much easier to maintain. Remember, victories are won and lost in the mind. Sin is first conceived in the mind. *Our lives become distracted because our minds are distracted.* It is possible to be at peace even amid a storm. We just need to keep our gaze on God and His love for us.

Study Time

1. Read Romans 8:6. What does this verse mean to you? Explain.

2. Read 1 Peter 1:13.

3. Describe the areas in your life where you feel you are thinking clearly.

4. In what area of your life are you not so clear?

5. Do you exercise self-control in your thought life? Explain.

6. How can you improve in this area?

7. What blessings are you looking forward to?

8. What blessings do you forget to think about? What can you do to remind yourself to look forward with hope?

9. Read 1 Peter 1:14.

10. In what ways are you obeying God right now?

11. Are you giving Him only partial obedience in some ways?

12. The last part of this verse tells us not to slip back into our old ways. What safeguards do you have on your life, your heart, and your mind?

13. Memorize Psalm 19:14 and Isaiah 26:3. These verses will help fortify your gates.

Personal Reflection

1. This week we're being intentional about guarding and redirecting our thought life. In what ways have you grown in this regard? (For example, my thoughts used to run wild in this area, but now I instinctively think healthier thoughts, and I'm quick to redirect my wandering thoughts.)

2. What was the catalyst for your growth in this area of your thought life (e.g., a crisis, God's Word, examples from other Christians, a sermon at church)?

3. What next aspect of your thought life are you ready to tackle and why? Write out a prayer asking God to empower you with His Spirit so you can grow and find new freedom in your thought life.

This Week's Goal:

_____

_____

_____

God's Promise to Me:

_____

_____

_____

What Keeps You Balanced, Grounded?

I seek God's face by digging deep in Scripture. I let Him determine the flow of where He takes me. I have to let go of my desire to control things. I take lots of notes. I write down passages of Scripture and the promptings of the Holy Spirit. I describe the word pictures or illustrations that come to mind. And if my thoughts wander, I return to my notes and take the time necessary to re-saturate myself in His presence. It's almost like I'm riding or surfing a spiritual wave with God.

—Rebecca

Thirteen

Spiritual Strength and Endurance

You have armed me with strength for the battle;
you have subdued my enemies under my feet.
2 SAMUEL 22:40

Since we are surrounded by such a huge crowd
of witnesses to the life of faith, let us strip off
every weight that slows us down, especially the
sin that so easily trips us up. And let us run with
endurance the race God has set before us.
HEBREWS 12:1

You've seen me refer to the time when I battled an illness while try-ing to raise three active little boys. Please allow me to revisit that season one more time. My boys were one, three, and five years old; I was in my twenties. Our house was falling apart and we had no money to fix it. We lived on very few groceries, I parented with very little strength, and our medical bills far exceeded our income. I could not see a way out. I struggled to find a purpose in it all.

I remember one particular day as if it were yesterday. I sat on our couch, which was tearing at the seams. I had holes in my jeans (before it was fashionable), and holes about to break loose in my socks. The boys danced to a song on *Sesame Street*, yelling and running from one end of the living room to the other. I envied their energy. My face was numb and my joints ached as I sat there.

Suddenly the phone rang. I stretched the long cord down the hallway so I could hear. It was an old friend. She said, "Susie, I know we've lost touch, but I've heard of your plight and have been praying for you. Listen to me: I believe the Lord is using your pain to build a platform from which you will speak someday. Lean into the pain and learn all you can from it, because you're going to have a story to tell afterward."

She shined a ray of light into my darkness. I was so buried under the heaviness of my situation that I couldn't fathom the possibility that God might use my hardship and heartbreak to prepare me for His purposes. But once I got a hold of the mind of Christ in my situation, the Enemy couldn't as easily bully me with fear and intimidation. As soon as my friend spoke those words to me, I knew they were true. I knew someday I would minister to women. In fact, my first speaking engagement took place within a year of that phone call. I was still sick, still poor, and still had holes in my jeans, but I packed up my little ones and went to speak to a mom's group about how I was keeping my faith during such a time of struggle.

Life got worse for me before it got better, and I battled many trials along the way, but I had in my heart a sense of calling from the Lord. I decided I would trust His voice more than the messages my circumstances consistently spoke to me. I'd read Scripture and circle the promises. I'd pray the Psalms, and I found great inspiration from heroes of the Bible like Joseph and Job.

Joseph had a calling on his life. God put a dream in his heart. But he, like me, didn't have the maturity to handle it in his younger years. God allowed Joseph to endure incredible injustice and heartache—trials that prepared him to rule with justice and kindness. With every unjust situation, Joseph yielded, trusted, and was teachable, and in every case he rose to a role of influence and leadership. Joseph's situation is described in Psalm 105:16-22. The passage says God sent him ahead, though it appeared he'd been left behind. You see, God is always thinking ahead and preparing us to meet needs further down the road. Joseph was sold into slavery, falsely accused, and sent to prison. He learned patience, humility, and obedience through the things he suffered. Jesus did too. "Even though Jesus was God's Son, he learned obedience from the things he suffered" (Hebrews 5:8).

We, too, will learn patience, humility, and obedience through the trials we suffer. When an old pastor friend of mine counsels people struggling through heavy circumstances, he first seeks God and asks Him the question, "Is it a sin or a test?" Some of the pain we go through we bring upon ourselves; other times God simply allows hard times to strengthen us. This is what's wonderful about God, though. Even *if* our struggle is because of sin, if we confess it before Him, He will, in His divine wisdom, use the consequences to do a beautiful, miraculous work in us.

It's important to note that we can lengthen the days of our struggle by our own lack of faith. The Israelites took 40 years to complete a journey that should have taken them a week or two. One commentary explained that their wandering through the desert was a consequence of their rebellious fears. Think about that. Fear can be rebellious. While God is merciful and understands when we're afraid, we must understand that if we cling too tightly to our fears, it is an affront to His love and faithfulness. "Perfect love casts out fear" (1 John 4:18 NKJV).

"The people *refused* to enter the pleasant land, *for they wouldn't believe his promise to care for them. Instead, they grumbled in their tents and refused to obey the* LORD" (Psalm 106:24-25, emphasis added). The Israelites' journey parallels our journeys. They were not made for captivity; they were made to live free. *We are not made for captivity;* we are made to live free. "You have been called to live in freedom, my brothers and sisters. But don't use your freedom to satisfy your sinful nature, Instead, use your freedom to serve one another in love" (Galatians 5:13).

Everything that binds us, ties us up, and makes us insecure is based on a lie. Oswald Chambers wrote, "We have an incredible capacity for

God, but sin, wrong thinking, and unbelief keep us from Him."[1] As we learn to believe that everything that comes our way serves a higher purpose, our faith will grow along with our tenacity to hang in there when life gets tough.

We are not made for captivity; we are made to live free.

Free to Dream

Do you have a dream in your heart? At my engagements, I sometimes ask women to tell me what dreams are hiding inside them. All too often they shrink back and sheepishly share dreams they think are way out of their reach. Did you know every one of us is called to a dream bigger than ourselves? Sadly, most people never do anything about their dream because of fear, lack of faith, or little desire to leave their comfort zone. But others listen to that inner voice, dare to trust in the God of big dreams, and venture out. However, before taking hold of the prize, they sometimes enter a time of humbling preparation, inner strengthening, and character refining.

As you look carefully at the components of spiritual strength and endurance, it's important to think about the direction in your life. God wants to lead you somewhere. He wants you to step out in faith. He wants to multiply your gifts *and* their impact. He wants to surprise you by showing up in impossible situations. He has a specific plan and purpose He's wired you for. If you haven't done this yet, go before Him and get a sense of what that ultimate calling might be. If you'd like to explore this idea on a deeper level, check out my book *Your Beautiful Purpose: Discovering and Enjoying What God Can Do Through You.* "'I know the plans I have for you,' says the LORD. 'They are plans for good and not for disaster, to give you a future and a hope'" (Jeremiah 29:11).

As we look beyond our circumstances with the hope and the knowledge that God is up to something, our struggles are easier to bear. When we know *and believe* that our hard times are working something wonderful in us, those struggles won't have the power to wound and disillusion us the way they used to.

Spiritual Strength Training

In the first half of this book, we addressed physical strength. We learned that when we lift properly, our bodies get stronger and our thresholds, higher. In other words, our capacity to lift heavier weight without injury increases. It's the same in our spiritual lives. God, in His grace, filters through His hands measured trials (He doesn't cause them, but He allows them). He knows our frame (Psalm 103:14 NKJV). He knows how much we can handle. "For my yoke is easy to bear, and the burden I give you is light" (Matthew 11:30).

I know that doesn't always feel true. It certainly didn't for me. Back in my days of back-to-back crises, I would often throw my head back and yell, "Lord, I think You have me mixed up with Susie Larson in Cincinnati, because this is *far* more than I can handle!"

I eventually realized that much of the weight crushing me was self-induced; it came from my own lack of faith, my fear, and my desire to have what I wanted more than what God wanted for me. Once I submitted my will to Him, peace came in, and I was no longer bent beneath my load. I've learned that in every situation, God has placed empowering grace and settling peace that are ours for the taking. We just have to want God's provision more than we want our own way.

Here are a few things to remember about spiritual strength training.

Heavy things make us stronger. "Search for the LORD and for his strength; continually seek him" (1 Chronicles 16:11). God allows completely painful circumstances and unjust people to trip us up and weigh us down. But in the shifting of our weight and the digging deep for strength, we learn love and grace. This is where we gain the spiritual muscle to weather the storm. We must refuse the weights of guilt, fear, shame, and condemnation, for they are not from God. Anger, selfishness, and unforgiveness are also weights that slow us down and diminish our strength.

In the first half of this book, I said you can get your body to do almost anything as long as you "ask nicely" and take a step at a time. Well, the way we ask nicely in the spiritual realm is to rid our lives of weights Jesus died for and carry only what He entrusts to us. Our

power and our strength come from God. We can stand up under our
load when we look for Him and find Him *in* our struggle—and then
believe what He says.

Resistance in life isn't without purpose. "In your strength I can crush
an army; with my God I can scale any wall" (Psalm 18:29). Every one
of us will face battles in life. Sometimes God allows "enemies" in our
land to teach us how to battle against the true enemy of our soul. But
we do not battle as the world does. We battle hatred with love, offense
with forgiveness, impatience with kindness, and pride with humility.
We cannot hide our heads in the sand hoping that no evil, betrayal, or
injustice will darken our doorstep. They will, and we must be armed
ahead of time with such an overwhelming sense of the love of God that
we are quickly able to put evil under our feet and walk on in love. If we
are not prepared, we will engage in a battle on a level we cannot win.
Our only defense is Christ.

"Every child of God defeats this evil world, and we achieve this victory through our faith. And who can win this battle against the world?
Only those who believe that Jesus is the Son of God" (1 John 5:4-5).
Whatever army rises against us, whatever wall stands in our way, God
has given us strength to overcome it. Sometimes He will allow us a time
of straining and pushing against something that will not budge, and
then suddenly one day we will step back and realize that in all our resist-
ing against the obstacle, we've gained the spiritual muscle to go over
it! "Such people will not be overcome by evil. Those who are righteous
will be long remembered. They do not fear bad news; they confidently
trust the LORD to care for them. They are confident and fearless and can
face their foes triumphantly" (Psalm 112:6-8). We take a strong stance
against the enemy of our souls and we take a humble stance before the
Savior of our souls. That's our sweet spot in battle.

Resistance breaks down old limitations and builds a new threshold.
"The war between the house of Saul and the house of David dragged
on and on. The longer it went on the stronger David became, with
the house of Saul getting weaker" (2 Samuel 3:1 MSG). This is a critical
point. Both David and Saul were involved in the same fight, but over

time one grew in strength while the other grew weaker. David walked humbly in the fear of the Lord. He fought the battles God called him to. He obeyed God and repented when he sinned. Saul, on the other hand, operated out of greed, lust for power, jealousy, and insecurity. He lost sight of the bigger picture and exhausted himself trying to rescue his sense of self-worth.

Women battle over these same issues. We grab for what we want, and when someone threatens us, we either get big and reactionary or we get small and passive. And no matter our personality style, we make an art of pointing out flaws in others while magnifying what we do well. God help us! When we come to a place of such assurance in the Lord that we clearly see insecurity, jealousy, and greed as things that *diminish* strength, we will be quicker to put them under our feet. As we walk in humble fear of the Lord, repent when we sin, and fervently battle against attitudes and responses that weaken our spiritual muscles and lessen our love, over time we will find ourselves stronger, more steadfast, and unafraid of the future. "She is clothed with strength and dignity, and she laughs without fear of the future" (Proverbs 31:25).

Atrophy. Remember the old phrase used to describe atrophy? *Use it or lose it.* The same is true in the spiritual sense. Not that you lose your salvation, because if you're in Christ, you're secure in Him. But if you neglect spiritual things, you will lose your influence and your sense of spiritual strength and agility. "To those who listen to my teaching, more understanding will be given, and they will have an abundance of knowledge. But for those who are not listening, even what little understanding they have will be taken away from them" (Matthew 13:12). Spiritual atrophy happens when we take a break from the things of God. If we put off our walk of faith for some other day, we will eventually become soft and weak. Every morning we wake up to fresh mercies and a chance to start again. Every day we're given opportunity to serve Him well and faithfully use our gifts.

Today we have the chance to learn more about Jesus, to spend more time in His presence, to develop the gifts He has given us, and to reach out to and love well those who don't know Him. Those who lived for

Him, who daily took their sins and frailties to the cross, who spent their gifts on a lost and dying world, and who kept heaven busy with countless prayers of faith...they will be able to look into their Savior's eyes and hear Him say, "Well done, my good and faithful servant" (Matthew 25:23).

Seek Him now. Draw all your strength from Him. Give faithfully and wisely of yourself and your gifts with the holy expectation that He will multiply your offering and lovingly replenish you. Stay sensitive to the Holy Spirit. Ask forgiveness when you sin. Keep heaven busy with your prayers. Take hold of all God has offered you, steward it well, and He will entrust you with a greater capacity for the things of God. Live a thriving, flourishing walk of faith. Keep stretching and working your spiritual muscles.

Keep the bigger picture in mind. "Don't shuffle along, eyes to the ground, absorbed with the things right in front of you. Look up, and be alert to what is going on around Christ—that's where the action is. See things from his perspective" (Colossians 3:2 MSG). Nothing is impossible with God, and overwhelming victory belongs to us who belong to Him (Romans 8:37).

Most times we're too close to our own story to see the bigger story God is writing in our lives. When you feel bogged down by your problems and overwhelmed by your fears, that's a perfect time to step back and look up. It's exactly the time to ask God to show you His strength and His affection for you.

Think about this: The God of the universe—the One who put the stars in place—thinks about you, intervenes for you, and answers prayers uttered by you. Take a deep breath and exhale, and pray your way through this beautiful psalm:

> *I lift up my eyes to the mountains—*
> *where does my help come from?*
> *My help comes from the LORD,*
> *the Maker of heaven and earth.*

He will not let your foot slip—
he who watches over you will not slumber;
indeed, he who watches over Israel
will neither slumber nor sleep.

The LORD watches over you—
the LORD is your shade at your right hand;
the sun will not harm you by day,
nor the moon by night.

The LORD will keep you from all harm—
he will watch over your life;
the LORD will watch over your coming and going
both now and forevermore.

PSALM 121 NIV

Jesus loves you deeply and profoundly. He's always "instantly" there for you even if He doesn't intervene the way you want Him to. And He is always calling you and me to a higher perspective than is natural for us. Make it a habit to look above your problems and view your life and your situation as one whom God loves.

Precious Lord,

You are the strength of my heart. May I never be afraid of the battles life promises. Instead, may I rise every day with a fresh awareness of Your power within me. Help me to face my foes with a courageous and humble heart. More than anything, I ask that You keep me constantly aware of Your love. It is far too easy to lose sight of who I am and what I'm called to when hard times press in. And yet this is when I most need to walk in the reality of the kingdom woman I am. I long to stand strong when the storms hit. I want to keep my eyes on You even when the waves threaten to overtake me. Everything I need is found in You. Help me to walk in a manner worthy of Your Name. In Jesus's name I pray, amen.

Steps Toward Health

- I will pause and remember the times God has been faithful. I will allow these memories to strengthen my faith.

- I will ask God for a fresh perspective on what is currently pressing in on me.

- I will take steps to strengthen my "spiritual muscles" by developing a gift God has given me.

- I will forgive whoever may be causing me pain or discomfort. I will seek God for help in this.

- I will refuse to let my circumstances define me. I will look to Jesus and allow Him to put fresh hope and a dream in my heart.

- I will not give up when times of preparation and testing come.

- I will spend some time with Jesus and ask Him for a bigger perspective on the battles I'm walking through.

Try This

- Write down what is currently pressing in on you. What's at risk right now (honor, reputation, provision, security, friendships, health)? Using a concordance, find a corresponding Scripture and memorize it. For instance, if you are feeling humiliated, memorize Psalm 62:7: "My victory and honor come from God alone. He is my refuge, a rock where no enemy can reach me."

- Pay attention to your thoughts and your gaze. Spend more time thinking about God's love and faithfulness than your current situation. You'll keep your peace by looking at Him. "You will keep in perfect peace all who trust in you, whose thoughts are fixed on you!" (Isaiah 26:3).

- Keep short accounts with your sin. Ask God for forgiveness the minute you realize you have said or done something you shouldn't. We are especially vulnerable to falling or failing during turbulent times. If we allow pride or ignorance to keep us from admitting when we're wrong, we give the Enemy an open door to do more damage than he's already done. God strengthens us in our battles when we stand fiercely against the lies of the Enemy (Ephesians 6:16) and we bow humbly before the throne of God and give Him full access to our character and our story. Jesus draws near to the humble in heart, but He distances Himself from the proud. "Though the Lord is great, he cares for the humble, but he keeps his distance from the proud" (Psalm 138:6).

- Pay attention to your growth process and be grateful. As we walk closely with the Lord and do what He says, we will gain spiritual health and strength. Take the time to notice how you're able to carry a trial today that would have put you under a year ago. Amid all our daily battles and struggles, we must take time to note our victories and celebrate our progress. Be encouraged! You're a work in progress, and you get to be!

Balance Application

Spiritually speaking, heavy things make us stronger if we allow them to. No matter who we are, we'll face battles in this life. But if we choose to take God at His word and trust Him in the hard times, we'll find our spiritual lives strengthened beyond what we imagined. As we remember that He works everything together for our good (Romans 8:28), we will have the courage to walk through storms that threaten to sweep us away. When we keep our feet firmly planted on the Rock of our salvation (Psalm 95:1), the raging waters will only prove to us that He is sufficient. Before attempting the impossible, we will wait for the call of God, we will expect resistance, and then we will choose to view our battles as preparation. We will keep our eyes on Jesus, knowing He is faithful. When hard times press in, our faith can grow and our love can increase; but for that to happen we must first ask this question: Is my goal to be delivered from my battle or to be perfected in love?

If my heart is set on the Lord and His purifying work in my life, I will grow indeed (2 Thessalonians 1:3-4). On the hard days, we will hold our ground; on the better days, we will take more ground. We won't give up what we've already gained.

Study Time

1. Read Romans 8:31. Who or what seems to be against you right now? Is it any match for God? Reflect for a moment on the fact that God is *for* you.

2. Read Romans 8:32. Think about what love cost our heavenly Father. Think about all He has provided for us. Why do you suppose it's difficult to believe He will withhold no good thing from us (Psalm 84:11)? Pray right now about any barriers to your faith.

3. Read Romans 8:33-34. Read it again. Read this every time someone rises against you. Has someone in your life intimidated or accused you? How many times have you rehearsed it in your mind? How much energy have you wasted on fueling the angst in your soul? Confess any sin you may have committed, apologize for any way you might be wrong, read the verse again, and trust Him to deliver you.

4. Read Romans 8:35-36. *Can* anything separate us from His love? *Does* it mean He doesn't love us when resistance comes our way? *Will* we continue to encounter trials during our journey on earth? Write down what you *know* to be true.

5. Read Romans 8:37. Despite our struggles, how do we secure a victory? How can you personally apply this promise?

6. Read Romans 8:38-39. Read it again. This time, read it out loud and personalize it. Replace "us" with "me." Pay attention to what you're reading. Hear the love, the strength, and

the passion behind those words. Allow this powerful promise to fill you up and strengthen you. This is a great passage to memorize.

7. Write down everything pressing you (each one on a separate piece of paper). One by one, hold them up and confess out loud, "Lord, I have worried about _____ for too long. I have decided to trust You today with the outcome. From now on, I will spend my time focusing on Your faithfulness." Take your time, get through each piece of paper, and then throw them in the trash, burn them in a bonfire, or stick them to a cross. This outward, symbolic gesture serves the Enemy notice and proclaims, "I will no longer look at my fears. I will look to Jesus instead!"

8. Read 2 Corinthians 12:9-10. Describe a time when you saw God's power shine through your weakness. Remember this principle: When we are weakest, He is strongest in us. Don't hide your weaknesses. Bring them before the Lord and say, "Father, here is another area where I need Your grace. Thank You for Your grace. And now I will walk forward in Your strength."

9. Read 2 Corinthians 6:1-10.

10. Read it again. Allow this passage to challenge you, inspire you, and give you perspective. Today, every three minutes, approximately one Christian is martyred for their faith. Pause and pray for your own situation as well as for your suffering brothers and sisters all over the world.

Personal Reflection

1. This week we're looking at how our battles will make us stronger if we trust God and allow Him to train us. What's one battle from your past that hugely and positively made an impact on who you are today?

2. In what ways have you had to unexpectedly persevere in life? How do you strengthen yourself so you don't lose heart?

3. Read Galatians 6:9 and James 1:4 and personalize the work of perseverance in your life.

This Week's Goal:

_____

_____

_____

God's Promise to Me:

_____

_____

_____

What Keeps You Balanced, Grounded?

Knowing when to step back, slow down, and rest when things get too hectic. On the flip side, also knowing when I need to pick up the pace when I feel stuck or unproductive. My body always lets me know when I've overdone it, and the Holy Spirit sets my tasks before me each day—one day at a time.

—Becky

Fourteen

Spiritual "Cardio"

As you have received Christ Jesus the Lord, walk in Him,
rooted and built up in Him and established in the faith,
just as you were taught, overflowing with thankfulness.
COLOSSIANS 2:6-7 HCSB

May the Lord lead your hearts into a full
understanding and expression of the love of God and
the patient endurance that comes from Christ.
2 THESSALONIANS 3:5

I have a vivid memory from my college years. I crammed myself into an old van with several other students, and we made our way home for a much-needed break. While everyone else seemed to enjoy back-and-forth banter, I retreated into a world of my own, lost in a Watchman Nee book. I can't remember the title; I wish I could. But I do remember how the book made me feel and how it charged me to think beyond the surface. Once in a while I'd put the weathered paperback over my heart, close my eyes, and silently pray about something I'd read. This godly man had profound things to say, and I wanted every word to fully nourish my soul.

Again, I wish I could remember the title of the book, because then I could find the passage that rocked my world and share it with you.

But I will tell you this: After reading a certain chapter, I felt overcome by a deeper understanding of just how shallow I was. I tuned out the noise in the van, closed my eyes, and within seconds I grasped truths about myself that were utterly painful to acknowledge. Like a fast-moving reel, the frames of my life passed before me, showing me that most everything I had ever done had been done with *me* in mind. Even acts of service were performed to rescue my sense of self-worth, or to look good, or so someone wouldn't be upset with me.

Only occasionally—rarely, in fact—did the reel slow down enough to show me a time when I had served or given or loved simply because it was what God wanted me to do. At the time my actions had felt sacrificial, but sitting there in that dumpy old van, in a deep state of prayer, I saw from heaven's perspective the richness and value of one act done simply for the sake of love. I was completely undone.

I put my hand over my mouth, utterly aghast over the depth of my selfishness and the impurity of my motives. It didn't matter that what drove me was my own pain, fear, and relentless insecurity. What mattered was that I was doing "right" things for all the wrong reasons. The Spirit searched my heart and showed me my desperate need for more of Him.

I didn't want to speak for fear that my next words or actions would spring from a selfish heart. For the rest of the ride I kept my eyes closed and asked God to forgive me and cleanse my heart. I could barely speak for the next three days. Every time one of my sisters tried to engage me in conversation, I broke down and cried. They thought I had a relationship conflict back at school. I couldn't explain to them that the conflict was inside me, within my own heart.

Thankfully, my break from college allowed me time to lean in and listen to what God wanted to say to me. I cried in my room. I cried out on the deck. I went for a run and cried with every step I took. Honestly, it felt good and cleansing. I felt no condemnation whatsoever. What wrecked me was God's holy and searching conviction. I felt broken over the reality of my selfishness. But this is true, and has been throughout my whole faith journey: Every time God sets the plow a little deeper in the soil of my character, I gain a deeper appreciation of how much He loves me, how committed He is to my transformation, and what He's forgiven in me. And with each phase of the journey, I find myself more passionately thankful for a sacrifice that covered my sin before I was even aware of its implications.

> God demonstrates his own love for us in this: While we were still sinners, Christ died for us (Romans 5:8 NIV).

For those three days, I spent extensive amounts of time examining my heart and bringing my need before the Lord, kneeling in humility, gratitude, and awe that the God of the universe would even consider having me for a friend.

> When I look at the night sky and see the work of your fingers—the moon and the stars you set in place—what are mere mortals that you should think about them, human beings that you should care for them? Yet you made them only a little lower than God and crowned them with glory and honor (Psalm 8:3-5).

Chip Ingram writes, "When people encounter the all-knowing, all-powerful, holy, and infinite God of time and eternity, they are so overcome with His glory and majesty that all they can do is fall down and worship."[1]

The verse at the beginning of this chapter (Colossians 2:6) tells us that since we have received Christ, we are to *walk in Him*. We lose our strength when we forget to rely on God's strength. Jesus is the air we breathe. He is the oxygen that fuels us to do what we could never otherwise do. He defines us, and our value will always and only be found in Him. If we believe we have something to prove, we will serve to get, not to give. If we believe we need more attention than we're getting, we will serve to get, not to give. If we believe we lack worth, we will serve to get, not to give. That's not to say we should postpone giving or serving in a sacrificial way, or sit back and wait until we're full enough before we share what God has entrusted to us. What we need, though, is to daily, moment by moment, offer ourselves up to God and ask Him to search our hearts for any driving ambitions, impure motives, or fear of man that compels us to attach strings to what we give away. Instead, may we ask God to bring us truth where we believe a lie, and to give us strength where we are weak.

When we allow God to deal with and purify our inner motives, our work for Him will have a much greater impact and be far more nourishing to a starving world than service (and gifts) given with mixed motives. Serving out of emptiness will indeed feed some; but serving from fullness will feed many more. In John 15:16, Jesus appoints us to go and "produce lasting fruit." He also reminds us that when we stay connected to Him, feeding from the love and the strength He gives, we will accomplish much. "Yes, I am the vine; you are the branches. Those who remain in me, and I in them, will produce much fruit. For apart from me you can do nothing" (John 15:5).

Why does Jesus tell us to *remain* in Him? Because we are drifters at heart. We wander from the very things that nourish our souls, and we forget the truth when the lie just feels truer. Furthermore, the cultural current of sin, selfishness, and wrong thinking threatens to pull us away from a life of faith. Every day the Enemy sends lying messages and orchestrates lying circumstances, all to make us lose perspective and second-guess ourselves. If the Enemy can't have our souls, he'll work overtime to destroy or at least diminish our stories.

So how do we remain in Jesus? We cultivate an intimate walk with Him. We daily confess our needs, our weaknesses, our hopes, and our dreams. We listen for His voice and we're quick to obey. We purposefully engage in a faith community and acknowledge that we cannot mature or grow outside of a Christian community. We nourish ourselves daily on the Word of truth, and we listen moment by moment to the Holy Spirit say, "This is the way; walk in it" (Isaiah 30:21 NIV).

In the first half of this book, I wrote this statement: *At the heart of true, lasting balance is the ability to read your health and your circumstances, and then adjust accordingly.* This is especially true in the spiritual realm. As you walk more closely with the Lord, you will have a heightened sense of your need. You'll know when it's best to take a risk and serve, and when it's best to pull back and get your cup filled again.

Ideally, you will make these adjustments daily, or at least weekly. If you suddenly feel completely overwhelmed or that your cup is empty, and you notice that your reactions reflect your lack of fullness, take that as your cue that it's time for a reset. Clear your schedule and change some plans, if possible. Use your time wisely and do what you can to get some quiet time with Jesus. He may just give you a verse or a moment of clarity. He may simply infuse you with energy to finish your day. He knows what you need more than you know what you need. Make time for Him. He'll refresh you.

> At the heart of true, lasting balance is the ability to read your health and your circumstances, and then adjust accordingly.

During certain stressful seasons, you'll need these resets often. However, in other seasons you may overflow with strength and endurance—as though there's a special grace and favor over your life. Be prepared. God will provide ample opportunities for you to share your fullness with others.

As you gear up to take your spiritual health to another level, here are a few things to keep in mind.

Tangible Tips as You Prepare for Spiritual Exercise

Take an honest assessment. Assess where you are in your spiritual health and your stage of life. While it is good to dream about where you want the Lord to take you, it's for your own protection that you also honestly look at every area of your life. Do you have young children? Do you have a rebellious child who requires more of your time? Are you caring for aging parents? How about your "inner cup"? Is it half full? Is it empty? Is it overflowing? Listen closely and God will faithfully guide you in the way you should go. He'll tell you when to run, when to rest, when to serve, and when to be served. We need Him every hour. We'll walk through seasons marked by favor and grace, and during such times, God intends to use us greatly. But other seasons batter us; the winds blow, the storms rage, and all we can do is wrap our arms and legs around the Vine and simply hold our ground. Thankfully, we don't need to consider such seasons a waste. God does some of His best work in us when a storm rages all around us.

But the point is that our availability will vary depending on our season of life. When we develop the habit of paying attention to what our souls need, we will more quickly discern our wisest course of action. And while it's good to be teachable and listen to wise counsel, it's essential that we get our marching orders from Jesus. People will always have opinions about how we should spend our time, but ultimately, we're accountable to God alone. Our need and our availability will vary throughout the days, weeks, months, and seasons of life, and that's just the way it is. Develop a healthy self-awareness. Pay attention to where you are. Keep checking in with the Lord—He will always lead you on the best path for your life. This will help you maintain a life of balance.

Ask nicely. Remember this tip from the chapter on physical health? When you take small steps and incorporate disciplines one at a time, you can improve your life in ways you cannot even imagine. Be content to start where you need to. Resist the temptation to compare your faith journey with another's. Walk, lift, and stretch just beyond what is comfortable *for you.* In other words, God will call you to carry certain things, and He will lead you further than you can imagine, but He does so one step at a time. Give yourself permission to be a work in progress. We all are. Just as no one could jump into your household and run it the way you do, you cannot jump into a fully developed calling without first being trained and prepared for it. Embrace the process. The journey is as sacred as the destination.

Leave the comfort zone. You are probably sick of hearing this by now, but that means you will remember it: *To grow, we must push beyond what is comfortable.* When God asks us to, we must be willing to take risks. To risk is to take the chance of failure, humiliation, or embarrassment. To risk is to dig deep and do something that would be easier left undone. To risk is to love or give something away, knowing your love may not be reciprocated. In light of this, think of all the ways Jesus took risks for us. He was willing to risk His reputation, His respectability, and His comfort, knowing He would die without many even acknowledging His gift, and yet He thought of you and me. His love for us compelled Him to take a gigantic risk so His kingdom would be enlarged. We, too, will be called on to take risks that seem beyond us. But He will be with us every step of the way.

Understand endurance versus change. Know when God is calling you to press on and when He is telling you to let go. The thing you are doing might have been God's plan to begin with, but maybe now He is moving in a totally different direction and you must follow. Sometimes we stick it out and hang in there with something God is no longer blessing or calling us to. The grace for the task lifts, and the "thing" begins to feel heavier and heavier. This is where some make the mistake of thinking it noble and martyr-like to hang in there, even though it is killing their joy, strength, and perspective. God seems to provide a window of time to get out and move on to the next thing He has for us, and *not* doing so eventually becomes disobedience through lack of faith. Those who stay put after the window has closed often experience a level of burnout so severe that they never fully recover.

On the other hand, sometimes the Lord allows everything around you to go dry, but still there's the seed of faith, the call in your heart, the promise in His Word that He will take your offering and multiply it for His kingdom. You *must* hang in there in such cases. Many leave just before their breakthrough arrives. It's important to differentiate between the two. Seek the Lord in these matters, and also seek wise counsel. The Holy Spirit will help you know whether to let go or hang on.

One more thing to consider: If *relief* is your main reason for wanting to leave, then you most likely need to stay until God says otherwise. My pastor used to say, "You're not free to leave until you're free to stay."

And if *comfort* is your only reason for wanting to stay, well then, you should probably gear up for a faith risk. Buckle up, because the adventure of faith will be worth it.

Don't give up what you've gained. "We must hold on to the progress we have already made" (Philippians 3:16). Remember this point? It is much harder to get something back than it is to maintain it. Use what God has given you. Hang on to the disciplines you already have. Use your gifts, and guard the ground you have gained in your walk of faith. Think about relationships, good habits, and skills. In every area of life are things that require our attention or we will eventually lose them. How do we give up what we've gained? A little at a time. We make small allowances here and there, and, at first, suffer no consequences. But just as we mentioned in the first section of this book, our lives will respond to the most consistent choices we make. If in the most important areas of life we are consistently inconsistent, disjointed, and unfocused, we will surely wake up one day and wonder how our lives imploded. In her book *Something More*, Catherine Marshall writes:

> Usually we think we deserve a "little fun" by a fling into sinning when life has handed us some injustice or when we have stuck faithfully through some protracted trial. A degree of self-pity joins the blown-up pride of our self-congratulation of having been so patient and reliable. Many of us have found out to our sorrow what a deadly brew this is. Our eyes are completely off Christ and on ourselves. Out of this little mess Satan has worked some great triumphs.[2]

Take more ground on the good days. You've also heard this concept several times, but when you have strength to give, help someone. When you have some extra time, turn it into a Sabbath moment and pray. Keep heaven busy with your prayers. When you find yourself in a season of ease, dig into the Word of God. Study, learn, pray, and serve Him with all the strength He provides. When you endure a storm, *know* that the Lord is loving and true and continue to look for Him in the storm. Soon you will find Him, and He will reward your faith. In every season make the most of every opportunity. "Be careful how you live. Don't live like fools, but like those who are wise. Make the most of every opportunity in these evil days" (Ephesians 5:15-16).

One more note on this point: When the Old Testament kings who feared the Lord experienced a time of favor, they often fortified their cities. They strengthened their gates. When you are in a time of ease, shore up your life; delve into those areas in your soul that leave you exposed and vulnerable to the Enemy. Pray Psalm 139:23-24, "Search me, O God, and know my heart; test me and know my anxious thoughts. Point out anything in me that offends you, and lead me along the path of everlasting life." Listen for God's correction and redirection. He wants you to be able to stand strong against a real enemy whose aim is to steal what matters most to you. Is it time, money, relationships? Fortify your life.

It takes energy to make energy. We learned in the first half of this book that, to improve our physical health and strength and increase our energy level, we *must* work out even when we don't feel like it. It's the same with our spiritual lives. At first, more times than not, we won't *feel* like being kind when we're irritable. We won't *feel* like giving to someone who doesn't deserve it. We won't *feel* like making a commitment to serve in a way that will cost us. But every time we die to our selfishness that we may live more like Christ, God will provide increased strength to do what seems way beyond us. As we step out, Jesus steps in. In her wonderful book *Come Away My Beloved*, Frances J. Roberts writes, "Where there is the activity of the Almighty, there are forces of Life continually working to produce within thee a measure of the life and health and strength which are in Him."[3]

There is no limit to what God can do through a trusting, yielded heart. As we lay ourselves down, every single day, and open our hearts to what He has to say (and then quickly do what He asks of us), He will trust us more and more with the honor of serving Him in miraculous, awesome ways. Every year we walk faithfully with the Lord, we learn how faithfully He's walked with us. We develop a history with Him

that we can point to, showing that we can look back in awe at the ways
He showed up, moved mountains, and used such imperfect souls to do
His work. Each year as we press on in His name, both in crisis and in
times of favor, we will gain ground and spiritual endurance. Read the
following quote by Rick Joyner:

> The athlete's endurance does not increase until he reaches the
> previous limit of his endurance and overtakes it. The same is
> true of our spiritual endurance. We can testify with Paul: "I
> can do all things through Him who strengthens me" (Philip-
> pians 4:13). In Christ we can never say "can't" to what He has
> called us to do. We can say that we "will not" or "did not,"
> but we can never say that we "can not." He has given us His
> strength.[4]

Practice good posture. As I mentioned before, it wears on our physical frames to slouch and hang our heads. When we stand tall, our core
strength improves. Plus, we look healthier and more confident. This is
even more important spiritually speaking. We must not cower, hang
our heads, or second-guess our value. We must remember who we are
and *whose* we are. If anything in our hearts would cause us to hang our
heads, we need to put this book down right now, confess it, and spend
a moment in God's presence, allowing His Spirit to cleanse us from
every wrong.

Have you read this verse lately? "If we confess our sins to him, he is
faithful and just to forgive us our sins and to cleanse us from all wick-
edness" (1 John 1:9). You have every reason to walk with a holy confidence that declares, "I belong to Him," and a humble dependence that
proclaims, "I have nothing apart from Him." Practice good spiritual
posture every single day.

Listen to your body. If we are in a season when we can give a lot away,
we especially need to pay attention to our need for nourishment and
rest. If we go too long emphasizing one lever (output) at the expense
of the others, we will throw our lives and relationships out of whack.

Conversely, if we are in a crisis season when we are taking in more than giving out, we will have certain days when we feel stronger than usual. On those days, don't be surprised if the opportunity pops up to bless someone else. Those sacred moments of blessing others amid our own struggle strengthen us for His service.

Practice spiritual flexibility. "We can make our plans, but the LORD determines our steps" (Proverbs 16:9). Before I ever had the courage to write my first book, I asked God to confirm that this was His plan. (I was such a woman of faith, I only asked for confirmation about 13 times.) Finally, when I knew it was His plan for me to write *Mercy in the Wilderness*, I sat down at my computer. And I sat. *Is this what writer's block feels like?* Absolutely nothing came to me, so I prayed, "Lord?" He whispered this direction to me: *Your neighbor needs you.* Being the spiritual giant that I am, I replied, "Huh?" Again, that still, small voice prompted me to go to my neighbor's house. She opened the door with tear-filled eyes and asked, "How did you know?"

After a sweet time of sharing and praying, I headed back home. I was stunned by what had just happened. Convicted too. That was such a reminder that in every season and with every task before me, I must always be listening, always be flexible, and always be available to do what He asks me to. Even when we have received clear direction from the Lord, we must never go on autopilot or assume the road will be straight. Often, while giving us the vision to go west, the Lord first takes us east.

Spiritual flexibility also calls for humble confidence. As Christ-followers we're never too small for big things, and we're never too big for small things. We follow a risen Savior who lived exactly this way. He gets to decide if our assignment will feel beyond us or seem beneath us, and He'll equip us accordingly. Spiritual flexibility calls us—invites us—to consistently step out in faith and to bow low in humility, no matter what season we're in. We must be careful to remember during times of favor and success that no service is beneath us; if we think it is, we have wandered away from the heart of Christ. In our seasons of crisis and seeming defeat, we must not look down or look away with self-doubt. We must look up and receive the strength He provides and accomplish what He wills as He leads. If we remain teachable and flexible, and understand that the Lord has the right to change courses and plans anytime He wishes, we will be prepared to move when He does. "Be dressed for service and keep your lamps burning" (Luke 12:35).

Every yes is three-dimensional. As easy as it is to say, "Yes, I'll do that," "Of course I'll take care of that," or "Sure, I don't mind doing that," we must remember that with each yes we offer comes a commitment of time, energy, and space. When our yeses pile up, we find ourselves stressed out and overwhelmed. This directly affects our health and quality of life. It's good to say yes occasionally; it's even better to pause, pray, look at our schedule, and talk with our spouse or a good friend before committing our time. Oswald Chambers once wrote, "The good is always the enemy of the best."[5] We can do a million good things with our time, but our lives will be much more peaceful and powerful when we do the best things for the right reasons. Check out my book *Your Sacred Yes* for more on this topic.

Don't go through the motions. We serve a living, loving, holy, and powerful God. If we've given our lives to Christ, they don't belong to us anymore. And while Jesus didn't save us just to slave us, He asks for our trust, obedience, and engagement. When we start to go through the motions, we disengage our faith, and when we disengage our faith, our hearts are no longer in it. And when our hearts are no longer in it, we lose our spiritual influence. God's love is what fuels us and gives us passion. If we've lost our passion, it's because we've forgotten about His love. If this is true for you, go back and read chapters 9 and 10. Remember again how much Jesus enjoys you and wants to fill you with every good thing. Allow your thoughts to be flooded with the fact that He loves you and has a specific plan for your life. Get back to the most basic and important fact in the world: *You are the object of His love and affection.* You are not summed up by what you do; you are someone He enjoys.

This Christ-life always starts with Jesus, and it ends with Him. So how do we stay engaged when we feel ourselves drifting? First we remember His love.

This is real love—not that we loved God, but that he loved us and sent his Son as a sacrifice to take away our sins (1 John 4:10).

Second, we allow that love to wash over us, heal us, and fill us back up again.

May you experience the love of Christ, though it is too great to understand fully. Then you will be made complete with all the fullness of life and power that comes from God (Ephesians 3:19).

Third, we engage our faith.

It is impossible to please God without faith. Anyone who wants to come to him must believe that God exists and that he rewards those who sincerely seek him (Hebrews 11:6).

When a man asked Jesus what he must do to be saved, Jesus replied, "That you love the Lord your God with all your passion and prayer and muscle and intelligence—and that you love your neighbor as well as you do yourself" (Luke 10:27 MSG). Start there. Love yourself. Love your next-door neighbor. Love your children. Love your husband. Love those around you and be kind to those who irritate you. If you take these first few simple steps to love those in your sphere of influence, you will change the world.

One more note on this point: I mentioned in the first section of this book that the more you invest and apply yourself to each exercise, the more benefits you'll receive. Again, it's the same in our spiritual lives, but in this case, the benefits we receive are far more significant because they affect this life *and* the life to come. The woman who prepares for church the night before by turning off the TV, putting praise music on, praying for the pastor and worship team, and asking God to prepare her own heart for what He has to say will get far more out of the service than someone who stays out too late the night before, wakes up late, and shows up with a foggy brain, only to be spoon-fed by her pastor. Try it once. If you're about to go to a concert or to a Bible study or to church or to visit a friend, do a little investing beforehand. On the nights your kids have activities at church, fast and pray that day for them and for those teaching them. An inexhaustible supply of provision is in heaven, and God longs for us to reach up and open a trapdoor to His storehouse.

God's Saving Work

Meditate on the verse below. Take your time reading it and allow it to nourish, convict, and inspire you. How can we be even more careful to put into action God's powerful, holy, and supernatural saving work in our lives? How can we obey Him with an even deeper sense of reverence and awe? By embracing and believing that God is at work in us, changing us, and giving us the desire *and the power* to do the impossible. We are more than conquerors when we walk closely with the Father.

You must be even more careful to put into action God's saving work in your life, "obeying God with deep reverence and fear. For God is working in you, giving you the desire and the power to do what pleases him" (Philippians 2:13).

Precious Lord,

You are everything to me. Fill me up with more of You. Forgive me for the countless times I gave or served only to get something in return. All I need is found in You. You are the Source of life. Help me to believe that every insecurity can be swallowed up in Your love. Oh, how I want to live a full and free life! I want to fulfill every last thing You created me for. Increase my faith, increase my love, and increase my capacity to know You more. Show me where I am called to serve, and help me lay down whatever You've not assigned to me. I long to live a life that counts for something beyond me. You've provided all

I need to accomplish more than I can imagine. If I'm doing too much, help me to simplify my life. Help me to do less and do it more powerfully. If I am not doing enough, give me a passion for Your kingdom. Nothing matters more than living life for You. Thank You, Jesus. Amen.

Steps Toward Health

- No matter how I may assess my current season of life, I will pause to ask God to show me what He sees. And I will humbly respond.

- I will bring my life and my schedule before the Lord and ask Him to inspire, convict, and encourage me where I need it.

- I will embrace the promise that no matter where I am right now, no matter how I struggle, Jesus thoroughly loves and enjoys me. He cheers for me when I get it right and aches for me when I get it wrong.

- I will *practice* good spiritual posture daily by remembering who I am and whose I am. Soon it will become instinctive for me to stand strong and remember who I am in every season of life.

- As I simplify my life and begin to enjoy room to breathe, I will be open, available, and flexible for whatever God calls me to. I won't sigh when my plans are interrupted. I will look at new plans as a divine redirection of my day.

Try This

- Memorize these two verses: "Search me, O God, and know my heart; test me and know my anxious thoughts. Point out anything in me that offends you, and lead me along the path of everlasting life" (Psalm 139:23-24).

- Pray these verses every morning. Pray these verses before you make a commitment. Pray these verses the minute you lose your peace. When you stay close to the Source, you'll know right away which choices, which words, and which commitments threaten to lure you away from your first love and passion.

- Remember, kids always come before ministry, and husband before kids.

- Before you commit to anything, always ask yourself why you're doing it and whom you are trying to serve.

- Never say yes right away. Think, pray, look at your schedule, and, if applicable, talk to your spouse.

- Seek peace and pursue it—always (Psalm 34:14).

- Intentionally choose to love those closest to you in a more active way than you normally do. Be creative!

- Always look for the sacred moments throughout the day. They are there for the taking.

- Remember that His mercies are new every morning and His faithfulness is great (Lamentations 3:22-23 NKJV).

- At the end of each day, as you lay your head on your pillow, make sure you've not taken any accounts against others to bed with you. Someone once said we must not have our list on the cross and our offender's list in our hands. God forgave us and intends to forgive through us. For obedience's sake and for your soul's sake, do the work of forgiveness.

- We bring pleasure to God when we live by faith. Ask Him, "Lord, what would You have me believe You for right now? Change in my marriage, virtue in my children, blessing in our schools, revival in our church? How do You want to expand Your kingdom through me?" Plant that mustard seed of faith in your heart, water it with prayer and a holy expectation, and see what happens.

Balance Application

To do what God has called you to will at times seem beyond you and other times beneath you. If you want to learn more about the focus and courage it takes to make an impact in your world, read about Noah and Nehemiah. God wants to accomplish life- and world-changing feats through you as well. Wait on Him and get your marching orders from Him. "A wise woman builds her home, but a foolish woman tears it down with her own hands" (Proverbs 14:1). Build with your eyes on Jesus and your heart set on obeying Him. Don't seek to be understood but to understand the Lord's plan and His love for all people. Seek to understand where those who don't understand you are coming from. Do what He's called you to—no more, no less. Be brave in your calling. Refuse bitterness and pettiness. Take care of yourself so you won't fall into the temptation of blaming others. Take seriously the calling on your life, and nurture all God has given you to accomplish it. Embrace the life you have in Christ. It is a priceless gift.

Study Time

1. Read Luke 12:22-24. What cares of life most occupy your thoughts?

2. Read Luke 12:25-29. What helps you not to worry? Write down your strategy so you'll have it when you need it. Jesus commands us not to worry. He knows when we worry, we're most vulnerable to the schemes of the Enemy. That is when we are most easily led astray, seduced, and tempted to take short-cuts. God wants us at peace. He has called us to peace. *He* can take care of everything we worry about, but no one can make the choice to fulfill the calling on our lives except us.

3. Read Luke 12:30-31. See? He will take care of everything we need; but there is a contingency to this promise. What is it? What is your primary concern right now? How is God specifically calling you to put His kingdom first?

4. Read Luke 12:32. Be nourished by the love in this verse. God loves to bless His children with gifts they could never earn or deserve. When we seek first His will in our lives, everything

else falls into place (Matthew 6:33). Is it easy for you to believe that He loves to give you good gifts? Explain.

5. Read Luke 12:33-34. Give whenever you can, love when it's not easy, and trust that God will take your offerings and multiply them to bless others and store up treasures in heaven for you. God's economy is beyond anything this world has to offer. In what ways do you feel inspired to give?

6. Read Luke 12:35-38. Take your time on these verses. Rid your life of distractions and attitudes He is opposed to. He could come back any minute; be ready and burning with passion for Him. Write a personalized prayer out of these four verses. Ask the Lord to help you be alert and prepared for whatever He asks of you. Psalm 123:2 refers to a servant girl who keeps her eyes on her mistress, waiting for the slightest signal. Be *that* ready.

7. Read Luke 12:35-38 again. Look at it from the other side. Imagine you've lived a life of passion for the Lord. Try to picture the Lord of hosts putting on an apron and serving you. Imagine the feast prepared for those who love Him. Describe how this would make you feel.

8. Psalm 116:9 says, "And so I walk in the LORD's presence as I live here on earth!" Memorize this verse and walk every day in the light of His presence. Pause and pray. Ask God to inspire your walk of faith.

My precious sister, this is my prayer for you:

Dear friend, I am praying that all is well with you and that your body is as healthy as I know your soul is (adapted from 3 John 1:2). I have continued praying for you ever since I first heard about you. I ask God to give you a complete understanding of what He wants to do in your life, and I ask Him to make you wise with spiritual wisdom. Then the way you live will always honor and please the Lord, and you

will continually do good, kind things for others. All the while,
you will learn to know God better and better (adapted from
Colossians 1:9-10).

Personal Reflection

1. This week we're looking at the importance of spiritual agility and flexibility, activity, and heart engagement. In what part of your life do you most tend to go through the motions? Why do you suppose that is?

2. In what part of your life is it easiest to keep your heart engaged? Why do you suppose that is?

3. Spend some time praying through Colossians 1:9-10 (adapted above) and write down what you sense God is saying to you.

This Week's Goal:

_____

_____

_____

God's Promise to Me:

_____

_____

_____

What Keeps You Balanced, Grounded?

I have learned the importance of asking questions of myself in every season of life. I value the input of a trusted mentor or friend or coach who will sit down with me and help me evaluate, get perspective, and live intentionally...If my priorities aren't on my calendar, I live at war with myself, and the Enemy beats me up in the process. My values drive my schedule, my purchases, my relationships, my volunteering, and so on.

—Pam

Fifteen

What Words Do

*May the words of my mouth and the
meditation of my heart be pleasing to you,
O Lord, my rock and my redeemer.*
Psalm 19:14

I used to be a gossip, back when I was a young mom. I am now in my fifties, and God has totally redeemed this area of my life, but many years ago I said things I shouldn't have, I shared what would have been better left unsaid, and I hashed out challenges with friends instead of taking them straight to Jesus and trying to get the mind of Christ in those situations. On the one hand, I cringe when I think of the words that came out of my mouth and never should have. On the other hand, I rejoice that not only has Christ forgiven me, but He has turned my life around. I pray often for the people who hurt or bothered me back then, and for those I hurt.

Over the years, as I grew up in the Lord, I more quickly sensed the Holy Spirit nudge me to close my lips and drop to my knees. I saw many situations change and improve from my prayers, where words would have only made a bad situation worse. Prayer changes a heart when judgment never could.

But it wasn't until *I* was on the receiving end of hateful gossip that I realized something much more profound. As I crumpled to the floor in a heap of sobs brought about by words meant to injure me, I sensed Jesus kneeling on the floor at my side with His hand on my shoulder, saying, *I know how you feel. I've been there.* As I sat up and wiped my eyes, I came to understand a couple of things. First and foremost, the Lord showed me that our process, our journey, is *holy ground.* It is sacred to God. Our areas of struggle, insecurity, anger, and inconsistency mean something to Him, and He handles us with the greatest of care. It breaks His heart when we trample on someone else's holy ground with heavy steps, loud sighs, cutting words, and manipulative behavior. When women act like petty, gossipy, stereotypical drama queens, it's an affront to a holy and sovereign God. And when Christians behave this way, we do great damage and give Christianity a bad name. "You realize, don't you, that you are the temple of God, and God himself is present in you? No one will get by with vandalizing God's temple, you can be sure of that. God's temple is sacred—and you, remember, are the temple" (1 Corinthians 3:16-17 MSG).

When we tear one another apart with our words, it isn't just a bad thing; *it's treason.* Imagine, if you will, a missionary ministering in a danger zone. Let's say that, in a moment of stress, she says something she shouldn't. Now imagine the following day the offended woman hiding in a back alley with a local government official who persecutes Christians. The missionary walks by and the offended one points her out and says, "There she is!" Wouldn't such a scenario shock you?

And yet every time we decide to be offended by another woman (that's right, we have a choice), and we begin to point out her flaws, her weak areas, and her deficits, the Enemy prowls closer and listens to every word we say. Imagine his rotten-mouthed sneer as he rubs his hands together. Picture him giddy with excitement to have a traitor on his side—one who will expose and speak curses (and not blessings) against someone who simply needs grace and forgiveness.

Don't pick on people, jump on their failures, criticize their faults— unless, of course, you want the same treatment. That critical spirit has a way of boomeranging. It's easy to see a smudge on your neighbor's face and be oblivious to the ugly sneer on your own. "Do you have the nerve to say, 'Let me wash your face for you,' when your own face is distorted by contempt?" (Matthew 7:1-4 MSG).

Moving in the Right Direction

Years ago we had an aboveground pool in our backyard. We were also volunteer youth pastors at the time. Whenever we had a bunch of teens over, we'd do the "whirlpool." The teens jumped into the water and, all in the same direction, "ran" as fast as they could in a circle along the outer edge of the pool. They created such a swirl of current that the water pulled down in the middle, creating a whirlpool. Then we'd count to three, and on three they'd all turn around and try to go the other way. The water smashed against them so hard it knocked most of them off their feet! Eventually, though, as they persisted, the water moved just as powerfully in the other direction.

The thoughts we dwell on and the words we say create a current all around us. We either invite the power of heaven in to influence our hearts and the world around us or we live defeated, scattered, petty lives in agreement with hell's desire for us. To change, we will at first encounter an unseen resistance. But if we persist, we will change the current in our lives. God wants us to be holy; Satan wants us to be catty. God wants us to be powerful; Satan wants us to be fearful. Someone once said, "God has a plan for you and the devil has a plan for you. You're the one who casts the deciding vote."

> The thoughts we dwell on and the words we say create a current all around us.

Today I have given you the choice between life and death, between blessings and curses. Now I call on heaven and earth to witness the choice you make. Oh, that you would choose life, so that you and your descendants might live! You can make this choice by loving the Lord your God, obeying him, and committing yourself firmly to him. This is the key to your life (Deuteronomy 30:19-20).

How shallow we can be when we allow small irritations to divide us. We must become purer in heart and stronger in love. How much grace do we have for others? How much forbearance? My friend Sandy once said, "I never get too excited about a new friendship until we've had our first conflict; then I know what the friendship is made of."

Many of us have become too soft, too comfortable, and it takes very little for us to take up an offense. Let's strive to be the kind of true friend who's willing to wade through more than an inch of mud before we turn back in disgust. We need to be able to handle a little hardship and still have much love to give. If this doesn't apply to you, praise God. Use your strength to pray for women who struggle in this area.

What does this have to do with balance? The Bible tells us that our *own soul is nourished* when we are kind, but that we *destroy ourselves* when we are cruel (Proverbs 11:17). Jesus said, "It's not what goes into your mouth that defiles you; *you are defiled by the words that come out of your mouth*" (Matthew 15:11, emphasis added).

Misspoken words have started wars, broken relationships, split churches, crushed hopes, and wounded souls. The Bible says in Proverbs 11:11 that "through the blessing of the upright a city is exalted, but by the mouth of the wicked it is destroyed" (NIV). A whole city is destroyed by the words of someone's mouth! And yet it is *through* "the blessing of the upright" that the world is affected for the better. Do you know what this means? Our holiness and godly conviction, our prayers, and our spoken blessings have national implications! In every sense of the word, God wants us to be "flow-*through* accounts" to send His blessings to earth.

As we consistently seek the mind of Christ and *His* perspective, we will—in due time—pray with power and speak with precision. We'll begin to see things as they are, and not as they seem. We'll move from being a people who *react* to circumstances to those who *respond* to God's promptings with God's heart for the offender in front of us. Henry Wadsworth Longfellow wrote, "Every man has his secret sorrows, which the world knows not; and often times we call a man cold when he is only sad." Before we judge, we must ask, "What must it be like for them?" "Make allowance for each other's faults, and forgive anyone who offends you. Remember, the Lord forgave you, so you must forgive others" (Colossians 3:13).

Reasons We Gossip

Below are several reasons women gossip. Take your time with this section. Search your heart and be encouraged. God's mercies are fresh and new every morning. Each day brings with it a chance to begin again.

Fear. "Fearing people is a dangerous trap, but to trust the LORD means safety" (Proverbs 29:25). We fight a losing battle when we seek to win the approval of all people all the time. We live in community with imperfect people, and even the best of them sometimes have a wrong opinion or perspective. It's not just a trap; it's a dangerous trap to care too much about what others may think about us. Do you want to be truly safe? Then walk in the fear of the Lord. As long as *you* don't gossip, as long as *you* don't judge, as long as *you* do what God tells you to do, then you will be safe, because as you submit to God, He will surely defend you. If you talk about others, you *will* get talked about. If you don't talk about others, you will still get talked about, but the difference is that you will be hidden in God and have *Him* as your defense. "How great is the goodness you have stored up for those who fear you. You lavish it on those who come to you for protection, blessing them before the watching world. You hide them in the shelter of your presence, safe from those who conspire against them. You shelter them in your presence, far from accusing tongues" (Psalm 31:19-20).

Anger. "Understand this, my dear brothers and sisters: You must all be quick to listen, slow to speak, and slow to get angry. Human anger does not produce the righteousness God desires" (James 1:19-20). Anger is sometimes hurt that's been festering a long time. As painful as it is, we must bring our disappointment and anger out in the open, before the Lord. The longer it stays hidden, the greater the damage to our souls. It's okay to cry, scream, yell, and beg God to make some sense of things. But then we need to forgive. When I wrestled through anger, it was like playing "hot potato." I'd toss my anger up to God, and within a few hours I'd find it back in my lap again. I'd toss it up again, determined not to hang on to it, only to have it land in my lap again. But eventually, the "potato" stayed up for longer periods of time. As I prayed prayers of blessing on those who had hurt me deeply, my heart for them changed and eventually the potato disappeared. If unforgiveness is in our hearts, nothing matters more than battling our way back to a place of love. Unforgiveness poisons our souls and chases healthy relationships and the sense of God's presence far away from us. "Do not judge others, and you will not be judged. Do not condemn others, or it will all come back against you. Forgive others, and you will be forgiven" (Luke 6:37).

No backbone. "Let your love, GOD, shape my life with salvation, exactly as you promised; then I'll be able to stand up to mockery because I trusted your Word" (Psalm 119:41-42 MSG). We used to tell our kids regarding their choice of friends, "Don't hang around anyone you can't stand up to." Great advice for us, too, don't you think? If we have a friend who intimidates us and repeatedly drags us into conversations we don't want to be in, we either need to seek God for a fresh dose of courage or consider spending less time with that person. "A gossip goes around telling secrets, so don't hang around with chatterers" (Proverbs 20:19).

Pride. "Pride comes before destruction, and an arrogant spirit before a fall" (Proverbs 16:18 HCSB). Truly, pride is just another form of insecurity. Pride drives us to either think too much of our gifts or to think too little of our value in Christ Jesus. Our gifts come from Him and our value comes from Him. We grow prideful when we lose sight of our humanity and His sovereignty. We construct a bloated, lopsided picture of ourselves, emphasizing our good points and minimizing our bad ones. Pride is the most hideous of all sins. It's the very thing that got Satan kicked out of heaven. The moment we think we are something on our own, or that we are better than someone else, we position ourselves against the Almighty. I mentioned this verse earlier in the book but it bears repeating: "Though the LORD is great, he cares for the humble, but he keeps his distance from the proud" (Psalm 138:6). Nothing would break my heart more than to puff myself up and put others down to the degree that the Lord would need to distance Himself from me. We all have moments when we slip into such a mindset, so it's wise to keep a close watch on our hearts, our minds, and our words. Walk in a holy fear of the Lord. "You rescue the humble, but you humiliate the proud" (Psalm 18:27).

Envy. "You want what you don't have, so you scheme and kill to get it. You are jealous of what others have, and you can't get it, so you fight and wage war to take it away from them. Yet you don't have what you want because you don't ask God for it" (James 4:2). We have a good God. The reason we don't have what we want is that we haven't asked God for it. Or maybe we've asked Him but don't want to wait on His answer. Maybe someone else is enjoying a breakthrough or blessing we think we should have. We cannot hold on to envy and gratitude at the same time, so the best antidote for envy is thankfulness. When struggling with envy, we need to begin thanking God out loud for all the things we do have. When we start naming our blessings, one by one, we'll notice all the things we've been taking for granted. When we humble ourselves *and* entrust our desires before the Almighty God, and leave them there, in due time we will see movement and breakthrough in our lives. Envy kills our joy. The joy of the Lord is our strength. We must ruthlessly rid our lives of any hint of envy. "So clean house! Make a clean sweep of malice and pretense, envy and hurtful talk. You've had a taste of God. Now, like infants at the breast, drink deep of God's pure kindness. Then you'll grow up mature and whole in God" (1 Peter 2:1-3 MSG). "A heart at peace gives life to the body, but envy rots the bones" (Proverbs 14:30 NIV).

Boredom. "No, we neither make nor save ourselves. God does both the making and saving. He creates each of us by Christ Jesus to join him in the work he does, the good work he has gotten ready for us to do, *work we had better be doing*" (Ephesians 2:10 MSG, emphasis added). Women who feel bored and unfulfilled tend to struggle most with gossip. When our lives have no vision or passion, it's all too easy to find fault with those who do. Women who have a sense of direction and vision *do* have faults like anybody else, but at least they're going somewhere and doing something with their lives. If we're really concerned about them, we can pray for them. Otherwise, we need to put that watchful eye on ourselves and allow God to call us higher and grant us a vision for the specific calling on our lives. We are made for so much more than we can imagine. "We are carefully joined together in him, becoming a holy temple for the Lord" (Ephesians 2:21).

Here is the critical point: We do damage to one another when we speak from an impure, mixed-motive heart. We must not misrepresent God with our words. God is love, and in Him there is no darkness at all. So when our hearts are darkened with bitterness, judgment, and a critical spirit, we need to close our lips, humble ourselves, and ask the Lord to renew our hearts. This is not a small deal; this is a big deal. Our tongues can destroy a city, a church, or someone's life (along with our own). For out of the heart the mouth speaks. "A good person produces good things from the treasury of a good heart, and an evil person produces evil things from the treasury of an evil heart. *What you say flows from what is in your heart*" (Luke 6:45, emphasis added).

I love these words from A.W. Tozer:

> The heart's fierce effort to protect itself from every slight, to shield its touchy honor from the bad opinion of friend and enemy, will never let the mind have rest. Continue this fight through the years and the burden will become intolerable. Yet the sons of earth are carrying this burden continually, challenging every word spoken against them, cringing under every criticism, smarting under each fancied slight, tossing sleepless if another is preferred before them. Such a burden is not necessary to bear. Jesus calls us to His rest, and meekness is His method. The meek man cares not at all who is greater than he, for he has long ago decided that the esteem of the world is not worth the effort. He develops toward himself a kindly sense of humor and learns to say, "Oh, so you have been overlooked?

They have placed someone else before you? They have whispered that you are pretty small stuff after all? And now you feel hurt because the world is saying about you the very things you have been saying about yourself? Only yesterday you were telling God that you were nothing, a mere worm of the dust. Where is your consistency? Come on, humble yourself and cease to care what men think."[1]

It's time to raise the standard! The verses below are ones I have either memorized or am currently working on; maybe they will help you:

Hear me, you who know what is right, you people who have taken my instruction to heart; do not fear the reproach of mere mortals or be terrified by their insults (Isaiah 51:7 NIV).

The LORD is my light and my salvation—whom shall I fear? The LORD is the stronghold of my life—of whom shall I be afraid? (Psalm 27:1 NIV).

The hearts of the wise make their mouths prudent, and their lips promote instruction (Proverbs 16:23 NIV).

Take control of what I say, O LORD, and guard my lips (Psalm 141:3).

I have hidden your word in my heart, that I might not sin against you (Psalm 119:11).

A wise woman builds her home, but a foolish woman tears it down with her own hands (Proverbs 14:1).

An unreliable messenger stumbles into trouble, but a reliable messenger brings healing (Proverbs 13:17).

In quietness and confidence will be your strength (Isaiah 30:15, my paraphrase).

Watch your tongue and keep your mouth shut, and you will stay out of trouble (Proverbs 21:23).

I will open my mouth with skillful and godly wisdom and in my tongue will be the law of kindness (Proverbs 31:26, my paraphrase).

The words of the godly save lives (Proverbs 12:6).

These next two verses fill me with such a sense of awareness of how much our words mean to God that they make me want to submit my every thought to Him before I speak it out.

I have put my words in your mouth and covered you with the shadow of my hand (Isaiah 51:16 NIV).

[He] carries out the words of his servants and fulfills the predictions of his messengers (Isaiah 44:26 NIV).

If we want our words to be a wellspring of life, we must stay close to the well. Our words will nourish and build up when our focus shifts from what others are doing *to us* to what God has done *for us*. And He has been good.

Lord of heaven,

Purify my heart! Grant me a new perspective and a greater desire to please You. You are all I need. Help me not to get stuck in wounds and hurts from my past. Life is too precious to throw it away like that. Please, Lord, bless every person I have ever hurt with my words, and help me to bless every person who has ever hurt me. It's not enough to speak kind words if my heart is fuming. I want a change from the inside out. Heal the deepest parts of me, restore my joy, and make me whole again. Redeem my past, refresh my relationship with You, and renew my resolve to love others well. I need You every single hour. I am glad You're right here with me now. I love You, Lord. Amen.

Steps Toward Health

- If any offenses are hanging over my head, I will pause right now, ask forgiveness where I need to, bless those who have hurt me, and accept God's mercy for my past.

- If I struggle with a critical spirit, I will get alone with God and ask Him what's hiding under the surface in me. I will continually bring this struggle before the Lord until I am free of it.

- I will regularly check my heart for bad attitudes, judgments, and criticism. As soon as I notice, I will bring these things before God. I am determined to keep my heart free and clear of anything that will choke out the fresh life I have in Christ.

- I will begin to speak blessings out loud. I will bless my family, my church, my neighborhood, and my enemies. I will even bless myself.

- I will sing more often.

- I will memorize Scripture. I will hide it in my heart and allow it to be the standard for my soul.

- Even when I blow it, I will not let it shake me from my secure place in Jesus. My identity is never up for grabs or changeable with popular opinion.

Try This

- When you're in a group and gossip starts up, confront the situation, redirect the conversation, or walk away. Just don't expose yourself to that kind of garbage. "When you run out of wood,

the fire goes out; when the gossip ends, the quarrel dies down"
(Proverbs 26:20 MSG).

- Ask God to protect you during weak and vulnerable moments
  when you are apt to say something you shouldn't. "Free me
  from hidden traps; I want to hide in you" (Psalm 31:4 MSG).

- Never trust *anyone* with words that shouldn't be said.

- Talk less and listen more. "Everyone must be quick to hear,
  slow to speak" (James 1:19 HCSB).

- Read Scripture out loud on a regular basis. It will change your
  life. "The word of God is alive and powerful. It is sharper than
  the sharpest two-edged sword, cutting between soul and spirit,
  between joint and marrow. It exposes innermost thoughts and
  desires" (Hebrews 4:12).

- Purify your self-talk. Pay attention to what you tell yourself,
  and line up your words with the promises in Scripture.

- Instead of negative, binding phrases such as "This will never
  work out" or "Things always go this way for me," make bold
  proclamations of God's goodness, such as "Thanks be to God,
  who always leads me in His triumph!" and "I am so thankful
  to be a child of God and know that nothing is impossible with
  Him!" Take hold of all that's been taken hold of for you.

- Use the eight gatekeepers from chapter 12 as standards for your
  words. Remember them? We are to fix our thoughts on whatever is true, honorable, right, pure, lovely, admirable, excellent,
  and worthy of praise. One qualifier here: If something is true,
  but there is no love in your heart, close your mouth and trust
  the Lord to bring someone along whose heart is in the right
  place. "The whole point of what we're urging is simply love—
  love uncontaminated by self-interest and counterfeit faith, a life
  open to God. Those who fail to keep to this point soon wander
  off into cul-de-sacs of gossip" (1 Timothy 1:5-6 MSG).

Balance Application

God has entrusted much good to us. And He's deposited a lot of good in us. Think of the countless church services you've been allowed to attend without fear for your life. Think of the people He has put in your life just to love you. Think of the beautiful sunny days He allows you to enjoy. Think of the sunsets that have taken your breath away. His blessings to us outnumber the stars in the sky. May we never lose sight of His love just because life gets hard sometimes. The world needs to see and hear and experience what He is constantly pouring out to us. If we hold on to useless weights, past mistakes, and old wounds, people will receive an inconsistent message of God's grace. Our lives speak the message that Christ's love heals every hurt, delivers every promise, and forgives every sin. Look at the following verse not only as someone who delivers a message, but as someone who is the message: "An unreliable messenger stumbles into trouble, but a reliable messenger brings healing" (Proverbs 13:17). Can you think of a greater honor than being a humble, reliable messenger of God's grace and love? Me neither.

Study Time

We're going to do something a little different for this study time. We'll take a look at a passage from Isaiah, using the *Message* paraphrase. I think you'll enjoy it.

1. Read Isaiah 58:7: "What I'm interested in seeing you do is: sharing your food with the hungry, inviting the homeless poor into your homes, putting clothes on the shivering ill-clad, being available to your own families." This verse expresses Christ's heart for those in need. Pause, pray, and ask the Lord to show you whom He wants you to help. Ask Him to speak to you about your availability to your own family. Write down what He speaks to you. Determine to *do* what He tells you to do.

2. Read Isaiah 58:8-9: "Do this and the lights will turn on, and your lives will turn around at once. Your righteousness will pave your way. The GOD of glory will secure your passage.

Then when you pray, GOD will answer. You'll call out for help and I'll say, 'Here I am.'" Look at and list the seven things promised to the one who tends to the burdens on God's heart. Don't just go through the motions. Pause and think about how your obedience would not only affect someone else, but your own life, too, because you decided to listen and engage in ways that deeply matter to the heart of God. What does God promise to do *in* you when you allow Him to work *through* you, especially in matters of social justice?

3. Read Isaiah 58:9: "If you get rid of unfair practices, quit blaming victims, quit gossiping about other people's sins..." Make yourself think about times when you've been unfair with your assessments. Maybe you've summed up someone else's suffering, and gossiped about someone else's sins. If you've not repented over these actions, do so now. Otherwise, pause and pray that God would heighten your conviction in these areas. Ask Him to make you more holy, just, and compassionate. Write out a prayer.

4. Read Isaiah 58:10: "If you are generous with the hungry and start giving yourselves to the down-and-out..." Write down the most recent thing you've done for the hungry. Write down a way you've helped someone who was down-and-out. Take a moment and lift those offerings up to God. Imagine the smile on His face. Ask Him to multiply your gift in the lives of those you blessed. Ask God to make you more aware of the needs around you, and then meet those needs as best you can.

5. Read Isaiah 58:10: "Your lives will begin to glow in the darkness, your shadowed lives will be bathed in sunlight." We live in a dark world, and yet you will *glow* in the darkness and *feel* the warmth of the sunlight on the darkest days when you care for the "least of these" (Matthew 25:40), just as Jesus did.

Write a personalized prayer asking God to give you a Christlike heart for the oppressed and the voiceless in this world.

6. Read Isaiah 58:11: "I will always show you where to go. I'll give you a full life in the emptiest of places—firm muscles, strong bones. You'll be like a well-watered garden, a gurgling spring that never runs dry." This is a picture of a strong, healthy life inside and out. This verse speaks of fresh life springing forth; of being a "flow-through account" for the power of God. Rewrite this verse in a personalized prayer.

7. Read Isaiah 58:12: "You'll use the old rubble of past lives to build anew, rebuild the foundations from out of your past. You'll be known as those who can fix anything, restore old ruins, rebuild and renovate, make the community livable again." If you keep your heart pure and stay close to God, you'll be used as a master builder, a catalyst to someone's healing. You'll be known as someone who can fix and restore and renovate lives. You will have clean hands, a pure heart, and speak words that heal. Make this your highest aim. Write down a prayer of faith, asking God for everything He wants to give you and everything He wants to make of you.

Personal Reflection

1. This week we're looking at the importance of the words we speak (and the heart behind those messages). Take an honest inventory of your words these days. Have they diminished or strengthened you?

2. In what ways have your recent thoughts led you astray? Write out a prayer asking God to help you reset your course so you can think on and speak what is true and powerful and biblical.

3. What's God been saying to you these days? What is He asking of you in return? Write down your thoughts.

This Week's Goal:

_____

_____

_____

God's Promise to Me:

_____

_____

_____

What Keeps You Balanced, Grounded?

I dare to ask God and others, "Where are my blind spots? What is it like to be on the other side of me?" Questions like these help us to gain perspective...If we establish authentic relationships in the calm seasons, they will be with us during the storms. Intentional investment in community and individuals will be the only things we can take to heaven with us.

—Pam

Sixteen

A Deeper Rest

*God's promise of entering his place of rest still
stands, so we ought to tremble with fear that
some of you might fail to experience it.*
HEBREWS 4:1

I have a feeling this is going to be a tough chapter for me to write. As I
sit here with my face in my hands, waiting on the Lord, asking Him
to show me where to start, I sense that He wants me to give you an
inside look at a time in my life I would rather forget. In fact, I think I
hear the phone ringing now. I'll be right back. Okay, I'm stalling. I'll
get to the point. I'm going to let you in on a time when I was so severely
out of balance that I'm pretty sure I was on the verge of a breakdown.

As I mentioned earlier in the book, I have been speaking at retreats
and conferences for years. Since the day of that phone call from my
long-lost friend, I've known that my calling is to speak and write to
women. God graciously and wisely kept my ministry opportunities in
pace with the stages of my boys' lives and my family's needs. I clearly
saw this as His provision and protection on my life. Still, I looked
forward to that day when I would be able to put more time into my
writing.

Finally, it looked as though that season of life had come for me. My
boys were all in school full days, and whatever hours I wasn't putting

into speaking preparations I was ready to put into writing. I knew with all my heart this was something God had called me to. I looked forward to every chance I had to sit down and write. I had met several important people in the literary world, and it seemed as though God was preparing me to take hold of my dream.

One morning my husband and I received a call from our pastor. We'd been attending a little church for about a year. We loved (and still love) our pastor and his wife. They are some of the most humble, God-fearing people we have ever met, and we were delighted by their invitation to meet for breakfast. There we were, sitting in the restaurant, when after some small talk, our pastor got right to the point. He leaned in and asked, "Would you two prayerfully consider running our youth program?"

I sat back in our booth somewhat surprised by the question. Kevin and I had worked with youth in the past. We absolutely love teenagers. We also knew what running a program entailed: time, time, and more time. Kevin and I looked at each other, and then he replied, "Well, we will definitely pray about it." I was sure they had the wrong people. Nothing in my heart wanted to take on a whole youth program.

God had confirmed His call on my life many times and in many ways. I saw Him do amazing things in the hearts of women at many of my engagements. The primary burden in my heart was to minister to women. If we took this volunteer position to oversee and run the youth program, would I still be able to book speaking engagements? And when would I write? I had waited so long to be in a season of life that allowed me time to pursue what God had put on my heart. I loved the idea of opening our home to teens, but running the entire program? Surely this couldn't be God's plan for me!

But as I bowed my head and prayed, as I asked God to show me His will, I was surprised to sense He was indeed calling us to do this. I didn't want to. His call completely crossed my will. But I feared God enough to know that if I ran away from obedience, I would just be running into the desert (or be swallowed by a whale). I had been a Christian long enough to know that one way to kill your intimacy with the Lord is to be slow to obey, to partially obey, or not to obey at all.

We poured our hearts and souls into this youth group. We got to know the teens and absolutely fell in love with them. We worked hard, and God stretched us. We saw Him move repeatedly in the hearts of these kids. Overseeing the youth ministry allowed us to have our own kids with us all the time; we held most of our youth group meetings in our home, and the boys were right in the center of it all. We grew in numbers and in strength.

After a year of youth ministry, the church leaders asked me to join the leadership of our church. I was honored, and after praying about it, both Kevin and I agreed that I should serve in this capacity. I am embarrassed to tell you, though, that eventually I also joined the worship team, I occasionally served as the service leader (the person who opens the service with the welcome and announcements), and I gave the Sunday sermon once in a while. I worked as a group fitness instructor at the time. And in addition to his regular job, my husband oversaw the church's building program, which entailed an extra 20 hours a week for about a year and a half.

Even with all these ministry opportunities, I still occasionally spoke at retreats. I was still a mom, still a wife, and still faced a mountain of dishes and laundry every single week. I had slowly, gradually—one choice at a time—spread myself so thin, I thought I would snap. My relationships felt strained. My perspective became skewed. My energy level was as low as it was when I was first sick with Lyme disease, and the sense of God's presence in my life came and went. I was desperate for relief, but it seemed far out of my reach.

What in the world possessed me to get involved in so many things? That question probably has several answers, but the primary one is this: I wanted to help. I thought since God had postponed my dream of writing a book, maybe this was supposed to be the season to work hard and fill in many of the gaps at our little church. I knew without a doubt that we were called there to serve. I also knew that if I had disobeyed

God and tried to prematurely pursue my dream by taking matters into my own hands, God would not have blessed my efforts. I knew this was a season when I needed to learn to lay down my dream and pick up my cross. Still, although God's yoke fits perfectly, I was nearly crushed beneath my load. So where did I go wrong?

I once spoke to a man who was unfaithful to his spouse, and when asked how it happened, he answered in the most profound way. He said, "I kept changing the rules, a little at a time." I'll never forget those words. I think that's what happened with me. I figured that because I was called to serve, I would throw myself into the task. I had the best of intentions and saw a measure of fruit coming from what I invested in. So little by little I added more commitments to my life—more than God had asked of me. And every other area of my life was forced to accommodate my unappointed output. As a result, I experienced weakness in areas where I once was strong. I spent far too much time on "output" and far too little time being nourished and on rest and recovery. I gave away all my time, and with it, my sense of peace.

One day I went over to my neighbor's house. I was troubled and stressed and needed someone to pray with me. As I sat at her table and described how I was feeling, she responded quickly by saying, "I know a speaker who teaches on this very thing!" I grabbed a pen and piece of paper, leaned in, and said, "Give me her name!" She poked me in the forehead and said, "*You*, you goofball." What a wake-up call. Years ago God had given me profound concepts to share on health and balance, and I wasn't applying any of them. Things had to change.

Balance Is Just the Beginning

One night I met a friend for dinner and brought with me a list of every role I filled. We put that list on the table, put our hands over it, and prayed, "Lord God, please give us wisdom and clarity tonight. Show us which commitments You are blessing and which ones You are not. Amen." We discussed each commitment in depth until I could see for myself what I had committed to out of obligation, for fun, or because I lacked the faith that God would care for me.

One by one, as the Lord led me, I cut every extra commitment from my life, with the exception of the couple of things I knew God wanted me to do. Since it took me many months of running at that frantic pace to see (and feel) the insanity in it all, it took some time to restore my life to a place of balance, peace, and rest.

This burnout season proved to be a catalyst to significant life change for both my husband and me. We were both exhausted, and our marriage was running on empty. So we stopped on our heels, stepped out of the rat race, and took inventory of our lives. We decided nothing mattered as much as our intimacy with God, with each other, and with our children. Those were our big rocks. From there, we asked God to show us what our God-given assignments were. We asked Him to help us respect our own limits so we could do life at a sustainable pace. We asked Him—who has no limits—to do the impossible in and through us.

We now look back after 15 years of applying the principles in this book, and we marvel at the fruit, the momentum, and the multiplication we've experienced simply by learning the secret of the abiding life.

Oh, how we miss the wonder of who God is when we run the rat race! Learning the basics of godly, balanced living *is just the very beginning*. Once we learn to appropriate biblical truths that make our lives more fruitful and run more smoothly, we've only laid a foundation for the greater work to begin.

We can see, hear, and be a part of what God is doing on the earth when we finally slow down and understand why we don't have to be running in a dozen directions. We can live from a place of fullness when we find in our souls the inner security that proclaims, "I have nothing to prove and everything to gain by keeping the main things the main things!"

When we are scattered and depleted, we're barely able to pray. When we slow down a bit (but not enough), we pray, but all too often the prayers are one-sided. We unload all our stresses at the feet of Jesus, and then we zip to our next appointment. Now, Jesus is gracious and merciful. He loves us so much that He will move in whatever context we allow Him to. But still, He has so much to say to us, so much to show us, so much to teach us.

Far more than a place to go with all our stresses, Jesus's heart is a place we can live from, draw from, and learn from. As we bring balance to our lives in a way that allows us room to grow, room to listen, and room to respond, we will see the blessedness of living a life with room to breathe. If we want to maintain balance, and if we truly want to grow, we must give God room to work in our lives.

As embarrassing as it is to admit and revisit my season of burnout, in truth, I am so very thankful that the Lord allowed me to exhaust myself the way I did. I learned a life lesson I will never forget. I will never again allow myself to take on more than God Himself has entrusted to me. I understand now more than ever that when I do too much, in the long run, I am not really helping in the best way possible. When I try to be all things to all people, I hurt my health, my relationships, and myself.

> If we want to maintain balance, and if we truly want to
> grow, we must give God room to work in our lives.

Overcommitment kills relationships and steals our joy. *Doing more* doesn't necessarily *produce more*. Walking closely with the Lord and doing what He says, does. In John 15:5, Jesus said we bear *much* fruit by staying close to Him (not by doing more; by abiding more). My husband now has a framed print on his desk with this Calvin Miller quote: "Lord, help me to remember that I can make more bricks in six days than I can in seven." Wise words, indeed.

Christ intends for our lives to be marked by His peace and power. Yet we walk in weakness—not strength—when we do more than Jesus Himself asked us to do. But when we do life in the strength God provides, we gain strength, we know joy on a deeper level, and we see more fruit than we ever could otherwise.

Here's an amazing truth: Kevin and I now manage five times the load we managed all those years ago when we landed in that burn-out season. But we do so with a good, consistent bedtime, extended precious prayer times in the morning, occasional walks with our dog, and enjoyable visits with our kids. We've learned the phenomenon and the wonder of respecting our limits, and then appealing to the God who has no limits. From that place, we've watched Him increase our offerings and expand our vision of what's possible for those who live by faith. We're still in awe at the thought of it. And we want this for you too! God's plan and purpose for you will always involve an element of rest and replenishment.

I wrote extensively about this idea—the abiding life and the fear of man that relentlessly drives us to take on more than God asked of us—in my book *Your Sacred Yes: Trading Life-Draining Obligation for Freedom, Passion, and Joy.*

When we give our lives room to breathe, the wonder of all God has for us returns like a breath of fresh air. God loves us. He wants us to be full of joy and peace. He knows that *when* we are full of these things, *then* we will serve Him out of that fullness. "When you come to him, that fullness comes together for you, too. His power extends over everything. Entering into this fullness is not something you figure out or achieve" (Colossians 2:10-11 MSG).

Lots of years have passed since my time of total depletion. Now I enjoy hours in God's presence and an increased capacity to understand His Word and His ways, and I have an overwhelming sense of what He's called me to in this season of my life. I've learned how to rest, how to say no, how to play, and how to enjoy God's daily graces. I've learned how to work hard with a heart of faith and offer it back up to Jesus at the end of the day. I've learned how to fling aside time wasters and toxic thinking. I've learned how to face down my fears with the truth of God's Word. And as a result, more power and focus have emerged from my life than I could ever have imagined. There is nothing like intimacy with God. *Nothing* matters more than our oneness with Him. When we make time for Him, we understand our need for Him, and then we hunger for more of Him.

If you're too busy to slow down and be filled with a fresh revelation of God's love and replenishment, then you, my precious friend, are too busy. No matter what season of life you're in, God has made you for Himself, and He'll provide a way to fill you with more of Himself. We all have work to do. And the more we have going on, the more we need His input in our lives.

That Place of Rest

Why not embrace a peaceful life if it's been provided for us? What's keeping us from swimming upstream if we have to, to get to a place of perpetual peace and rest? Through my own experience I learned spiritual rest isn't a luxury or simply a benefit of being a Christian; it's a mandate from our holy and powerful God. We are warned in Hebrews that if we don't enter the rest God has for us, we will fall. "There is a special rest still waiting for the people of God. For all who have entered into God's rest have rested from their labors, just as God did after creating the world. So let us do our best to enter that rest. But if we disobey God, as the people of Israel did, we will fall" (Hebrews 4:9-11).

Why do we make sure our kids get to bed at a decent time night after night? It's because if they wear down, they will melt down. They'll get sick, lose perspective, and won't be able to function in a healthy way. It's the same with us. God is our Father, and He knows if we don't rest, we will fall apart. We will fall into bad habits, shortcuts, temptations, and sickness. We will fall out of earshot of His voice and miss the wisdom our day requires. Instead of gaining more ground and pursuing *increased* health and fruitfulness, we will *lose* ground—and with it our peace, our strength, and our effectiveness.

In previous chapters we touched lightly on Sabbath moments and Sabbath days. Now we'll look at two more aspects of rest. What I want to accomplish in this chapter is a whole shift in perspective. We *must* get out of the rat race. We must resist the frantic, harried lifestyle our culture has come to embrace. It's not good for our health, our families, or the health of the church. What God supplies is far better.

Sabbath seasons. In some seasons in your life, God may lead you *not* to be involved in any defined ministry *for the purpose of* healing, training, refining, rest, and seeking a deeper relationship with Him.

During such times you will spend extended hours in quiet, in study, and in prayer. For a time you will pull back from much of your outward activity so more energy can go into strengthening and deepening your spiritual roots. Of course, this doesn't mean you rest from serving the Lord. You can still go to church or to the grocery store or walk through your neighborhood and find someone who needs a blessing. As a child of God, you will always have the high privilege of being at His service. "All must give as they are able, according to the blessings given to them by the LORD your God" (Deuteronomy 16:17).

A Sabbath heart. "Those who live in the shelter of the Most High will find rest in the shadow of the Almighty. This I declare about the LORD: He alone is my refuge, my place of safety; he is my God, and I trust him" (Psalm 91:1-2). This psalm says it better than I ever could. Look at the first part of the first verse. When we set up camp under the protection of the Most High God, we will be able to rest there. When we *live* closely with the Lord, we can *rest* in His *shadow.* Imagine Him hovering over us, protecting all who come to Him for refuge. When we quit trying to control everything and everybody in our lives, and instead entrust our cares to God, He will lift them from our shoulders. When storm clouds hover overhead, circumstances heat up, or people ask for too much, we will not allow these things to lure us out of His shadow.

Instead, we will stay in that hidden place of rest, trust, and pray, "Lord, I see these things coming at me, threatening to disrupt the peace I have in You. Would You hold these things for me? Would You show me what's mine and what's Yours and grant me Your wisdom and perspective? I want to stay hidden with You. I know You are strong and powerful, so I will refuse to worry or be anxious. I will look to You to carry the world on Your shoulders while I rest and trust in Your glorious strength. I, like the psalmist, trust You." This doesn't mean you won't have to rise to the challenge of difficult circumstances or demanding people, but you can do so with a heart that refuses to enter into the stressful intensity of the age. God has called us to peace. "He will rescue you from every trap and protect you from deadly disease. He will cover you with his feathers. He will shelter you with his wings. His faithful promises are your armor and protection" (Psalm 91:3-4). We have every reason to trust in Him. The lie of the age is that God is not for us. Satan works tirelessly to steal our assurance and our peace. We must fight for it. And, sister, this is a battle worth fighting.

Father God,

You've already offered me far more than I could ever fully apprehend. I'm overwhelmed by the gift of Your Son. Every morning I wake up to fresh mercies, fresh nourishment, and fresh power from above. Help me to find that sacred place of rest in You, and when I find it, help me to set up camp there. Help me to live there. I long to please You with my faith; a faith that declares, "My God is for me, who can stand against me?" There is so much more You want to pour into me. Help me, Lord, to slow down long enough to receive it. Oh, how I love You. Increase my hunger and desire for Your presence. You are everything to me. Amen.

Steps Toward Health

- I will make a point to slow down this week. I will cut something out of my schedule if I have to. I will use that time to sit and reflect in God's presence.

- I will get up a little earlier in the morning to spend time with God. I will "ask nicely" by getting up ten minutes earlier each day this week so my body can get used to the change. I will remember that any time I set aside for God will eventually produce supernatural results.

- I will daily (hourly, if necessary) hand over my worries and cares to the Lord. I will diligently seek the peace and rest He provides.

- I will put "a restful, peaceful heart" at the top of my prayer list for myself, my loved ones, and even for my enemies.

- I will memorize Scripture relating to rest and peace. I will use God's Word as my weapon against the threats and harassments of the devil.

Here are a few to help you get started:

- "My soul finds rest in God, my salvation comes from him" (Psalm 62:1 NIV). Two things stand out to me with this verse. My soul is to find rest in God. Not when all my relationships are running smoothly, when my checkbook balances perfectly, or when, at the moment, everybody seems to like me. No, I find my rest only in the *fact* that God is enough for me without everything else. The other thing that stands out is this: If I can trust Him for my salvation, surely I can trust Him with every lesser thing.

- "Return to your rest, my soul, for the LORD has been good to you" (Psalm 116:7 NIV). If we've been lured out of our rest, we simply need to recall once again all the ways God has been faithful. Then we proclaim, "And my God will be faithful again."

- "Let the peace of Christ rule in your hearts, since as members of one body you were called to peace. And be thankful" (Colossians 3:15 NIV). What strikes me in this verse is the word *let*. God daily pours Himself out to us, and our call is to receive what He offers. This past year I had pastor and author Daniel Henderson on my show, and he said the best thing. He said, "The kingdom of God is not something we achieve; it's something we receive." Love that! As we open ourselves up to God's influence and perspective, His peace will rule our hearts because we'll look at life with God in mind. This point also bears repeating: Practice sincere, wholehearted gratitude in all seasons.

Try This

- *Spend a portion of your quiet time in total silence.* Linger over a certain passage of Scripture. Fix your thoughts on God and

His ability to speak the mountains into existence and to stir up the waters by the very sound of His voice. Rest assured that the Guardian of your soul is strong and mighty. At first your thoughts may wander, but stick with it. It takes practice, but the payoff is priceless. Giving God time and space to speak to your heart and to bring direction and even correction when needed opens the doorway to immeasurable peace and understanding. Read these wonderful verses: Isaiah 30:18, 40:31, and 64:4.

- *Write down some of the things the Lord speaks to you during this time.* Reflect on them the following day. Sometimes you will gain more clarity a day later.

- *Examine your heart throughout the day.* As soon as you notice a lack of peace or increased anxiety, retrace your steps until you find which thought or circumstance disrupted your peace. Often those instances are symptomatic of some deeper issues God wants to get at in our lives. He wants to deliver us of anything the Enemy can use against us.

- *Let your children see you commit yourself daily to the Lord.* Pray with them before meals, before they go to school, before a doctor appointment, or after you've had the privilege of purchasing groceries. Let it be commonplace to thank God for a good report from the doctor, for food in the cupboard, or for protection on the road. Allow them to see you bring God into every avenue of your life.

- *Be careful with your "anxious confessions."* If your children hear you worrying out loud, they'll pick up on it. More often than not, allow them to hear statements of faith coming from your mouth.

- Daily confess, "Lord, You are strong and You love me. I will trust in You today."

Balance Application

It really is a matter of belief. Will God come through for me if I put more on His shoulders than I put on my own? A certain feeling says if we don't worry about everything, we'll get lackadaisical and our lives will fall apart. On the contrary, the kind of rest we are called to has a focus and purpose to it. When we live in the shelter of the Most High, we have a front-row seat to see with our spiritual eyes and hear with our spiritual ears what God is doing in the world, in the hearts of our loved ones, and in our own lives. We are far more effective living close to the Source with a heart of rest than we are running in a thousand directions amid the clamor of the world. We are representatives of the Most High God and yet fully human. We need our physical rest, we need occasional extended bouts of spiritual rest, and we need to live from a heart that fully trusts and fully rests in its Almighty Father. It's impossible for Him to fail you!

Study Time

1. Read Psalm 84:1-2. Read it again, but this time read aloud with a heart of passion.

2. How uncomfortable was that for you? Mark this spot in your Bible and come back to it again and again, reading this passage out loud until your passionate words match the cry of your heart.

3. Read Psalm 84:3-4. Think about how all of nature recognizes the Lord. Life flows from Him and finds its place of rest in His presence. Why are those who dwell in God's presence blessed (happy)? Write down some of your thoughts.

4. Read Psalm 84:5-7. We will pass through valleys and storms. But more important than our circumstances is that we are headed somewhere. We are on a pilgrimage, heading toward a promise. And as we venture out, determined to follow our Lord when it's popular and when it isn't, we will find strength

and pools of blessing where there were none. What have been the highs and lows of your journey? Write them down. Remember, you are strong in the Lord.

5. Read Psalm 84:8-10. Notice the persistence and passion in this prayer. Sometimes we need to press in until we get a breakthrough. The psalmist was after something here. He was determined to find his hidden place with the Lord because he knew what was waiting for him. Have you experienced such sweetness in God's presence that you can honestly say, "Better is one day in Your courts than a thousand elsewhere"? If your answer is yes, I pray your experience compels you to draw nearer still. If your answer is no, you are in for a treat. Wherever you are, write down a prayer for increased passion for the presence of God.

6. Read Psalm 84:11. Countless treasures are available for those who walk closely with the Lord. Write down the five treasures listed in this verse, but leave a little space. Now expound on each of the five. How do these blessings affect you personally?

7. Read Psalm 84:12. Why does blessing come to the one who trusts in the Lord? Explain it the best you can.

8. Read Psalm 62:5-6. Write out these verses in a personalized prayer of faith.

Personal Reflection

1. This week we're looking at the importance of cultivating a heart at rest and a heart at peace. What life adjustments could you make to create more space in your life for rest and reflection?

2. Can you think of commitments you've made that you now regret? Commitments you know were driven by something other than God's invitation to you? Write those down.

3. Spend some time with the Lord. Ask Him for wisdom. What do you sense He's asking of you in return? Write down your thoughts.

This Week's Goal:

_____

_____

_____

God's Promise to Me:

_____

_____

_____

What Keeps You Balanced, Grounded?

I get out of balance when I fail to recognize that I'm trying to do too much. I need to stop and be mindful of how I'm spending my time. It can be hard because I may have to decide between several things I love to do or people I want to spend time with.

—Leslie

Seventeen

A Focused Life

The gatekeeper opens the gate to him and the sheep recognize his voice. He calls his own sheep by name and leads them out. When he gets them all out, he leads them and they follow because they are familiar with his voice.

JOHN 10:3-4 MSG

"S he would like to see you now," Bob said softly over the phone. I looked up at Kevin, who nodded toward the door. We drove in silence. Kevin sped up in hopes we'd get to her quickly, and then he slowed down as if to put off for a bit what we were about to see.

We entered the house and went up the stairs to the living room. All of Peggy's knickknacks had gathered dust. When I excused myself to use the restroom, I walked by the kitchen and noticed dishes piled in the sink, and her famous cookie jar was empty. Her hospital bed took up most of the room. Her frail body rested motionless under the sheet. With her head turned to the side, I could see that her eyes were partially open. Saliva ran from the side of her mouth as she labored to breathe.

I forced back the lump in my throat and scooted closer to this amazing woman of God. I gently reached over the bed railing to touch her arm. Her skin tore like a wet napkin. I quickly looked up at the nurse and gasped. "I'm so sorry!" The nurse reassured me. "Peggy can't feel much of anything right now, but it would be best if you just touched her fingers and looked into her eyes when you speak to her."

My mentor was dying. She had throat cancer, which had spread to other parts of her body. I was sick at the same time with Lyme disease. She'd so often minister to me as if I were sicker than she was. When I couldn't handle it anymore and cried out to God on her behalf, she would touch my hand to quiet me. With courage and confidence, Peggy assured me, "My Lord will take me when He gets more glory from my death than He does from my life."

Beautiful, lovely Peggy was preparing to meet Jesus. I would miss her terribly. "I love you, Peggy, and I always will." I sucked in a sob and continued. "You have taught me many things...I want to be just like you...Jesus is getting your place all ready for you. I love you so much." I wept as her eyes pierced my soul and her body lay perfectly still. When Kevin stepped in front of her gaze, she moved her head slightly and mouthed two words to him. We all stepped in to hear what was important enough for her to spend such precious energy.

She curled her fingertips around his hand and opened her eyes a little wider. Again she mouthed the words, "Love her." Peggy knew I was weak and would need Kevin's strength in the days ahead. My hands covered my mouth and tears came like a flood. I needed to wail. Kevin wrapped his hands around her frail fingers and said, "I promise, Peggy. I will forever." That was the last time I saw my mentor and friend Peggy Pearson.

Peggy was a woman after God's own heart. She was more like Jesus than even her husband, Bob, knew, and he loved her immensely. A flood of people came to the funeral and squeezed into the sanctuary. Bob didn't know many of these people, and yet they came. They came to pay tribute to a woman who had blessed them. She gave gifts to complete strangers, but told no one. Not even Bob.

"I met Peggy on a bus and didn't have money for lunch. Peggy fed me."

"I met Peggy at the hospital, and she bought me a cup of coffee and listened to my story."

"Peggy brought me many meals when my husband lost his job."

One by one people got in line to share their stories of how Peggy touched their lives and pointed them to Jesus. Bob stood there with tears streaming down his face as he learned that his wife was even lovelier than he knew.

Peggy lived the abiding life. In other words, she stayed close to her Father's heart. She embraced the truth that Christ was the source of all she would ever need. Through every season of her life—in her waiting and in her suffering—she never doubted the *goodness* of God. Peggy was a spiritual giant, though to the world she looked like a frail, aging woman.

In Psalms we learn God is not impressed with our strength or success. Such things are puny in His sight. What He delights in, what makes His heart beat faster, is someone who honors Him and continually trusts in His *unfailing love*; especially when the storms come (Psalm 147:10-11). To trust is costly, but anything worth pursuing always is. Jesus told us the water He gives would allow us to never thirst again. His water is pure and fresh and new (John 4:14). Yet we continue to dig our own wells and drink muddy water because sometimes it just seems easier (Jeremiah 2:13).

Peggy knew this world was not her home, and she lived like someone who was just passing through. She hung all her hopes and dreams on heaven's door and knew they were safe there. Her value, identity, and motivation were fueled by a love that surpassed anything the earth had to offer. Peggy held much of what she owned with an open hand because she understood the limitations of her earthly treasures. But she clung tightly to her precious Savior, knowing her kingdom investment was a sound one.

I pray that we can live like Peggy did. When we're lonely, may we wait for and believe God for the one He's preparing for us. When we're hurting, may our medication be the healing balm of His precious blood. When we're angry with someone, may our retaliation be a fierce prayer of blessing on their behalf. When we're excited, may we not get ahead of God, but rather take our every cue from Him.

This is the living, breathing fellowship of the abiding life.

Instead of digging our little makeshift wells that will surely fail us and sour our appetites, let us stay close to the living water of Christ, be nourished and replenished by Him, and trust Him with all that we need. May we determine *not* to live on fast food when He has prepared a feast for us.

Lord, help us to stay close to You!

What Is Your Focal Point?

When I was a young gymnast, I learned the main component of balance: focus. I could walk swiftly and leap on a balance beam. I could do cartwheels and back walkovers and turns, as long as I focused on one single point. As I fixed my eyes on the end of the beam, I could make difficult moves look easy, I could walk straight without bobbling, and I could get off the beam in one piece.

As we live with the end (eternity) in mind and we fix our eyes heavenward on Jesus, we will live in a way that makes difficult moves look easy, we will run and not stumble, and we will get there in one piece. We're tempted to worry about many things, but the only thing to truly concern ourselves with is keeping our hearts set on the Lord Jesus.

In Luke 10, Mary and Martha welcomed Jesus into their home. Both wanted to be near Him; both wanted to serve Him. Martha hurried to-and-fro, stressing about the *food* when the *Source* of all life was sitting in her living room. Mary, on the other hand, sat at Jesus's feet and soaked in everything He had to say. Martha complained to Jesus and asked Him to talk to Mary. And this was His reply: "'My dear Martha, you are worried and upset over all these details! There is only one thing worth being concerned about. Mary has discovered it, and it will not be taken away from her'" (Luke 10:41-42).

Only *one thing* is worth being concerned about. Jesus said this, knowing our pace of life would spin out of control. Especially for this reason, He has called us to His side. Mary wasn't scolded for not helping; she was praised for keeping her eyes on Him. Living an abiding life means we sometimes let go of certain things so we can do the *one thing*.

I've noticed in my own life, that when I leave undone the lesser for the sake of the greater, God multiplies my time and I usually get the lesser done also. And I did so without forsaking the most important thing. In the psalms, David also understood the call: "The one thing I ask of the LORD—the thing I seek most—is to live in the house of the LORD all the days of my life, delighting in the LORD's perfections and meditating in his Temple" (Psalm 27:4).

Dear sister, this is at the very core of a healthy life and a heart at rest—a life *focused* on the Lord, a life *absorbed* with the love that pours out of heaven daily, a life *fully committed* to doing what God asks. Our lives in Christ—lives well lived—will go from strength to strength, from glory to glory, and shine ever brighter until the full light of day (Proverbs 4:18). This is the life of spiritual balance: a life that centers on and draws from heaven's love. This love is never stagnant. It is always growing, always refining, and always dealing with sin and healing pain. It is always flowing in, making a difference, and then flowing out to a lost and dying world. Take Him in, make *Him* your focus, and see what love will do.

> Our lives in Christ—lives well lived—will go from strength to strength, from glory to glory, and shine ever brighter until the full light of day.

Precious Jesus,

Help me to rid my life of anything that needlessly hinders my progress in You. Nothing is worth more than You. Nothing compares to You. Fan the flame of love in my heart so I can better comprehend Your love for me and for those around me. I long to live a focused, abiding life. At the end of time here on earth, I want it said, "This was a woman who loved Jesus first and foremost." Oh Lord, kindle that kind of love in my heart. Help me to gain victory over every selfish sin, every bad habit, and every lying thought. I long to live a blameless life before You, and I know this is a noble pursuit. Protect me from arrows of discouragement and doubt. Help me to use my shield of faith to shut down the devil's every attempt to lure me from my place of peace. I am Yours. I will set up camp right next to You. Oh, how I love You! Amen.

Steps Toward Health

- I will wake up every day and ask God to give me a heart set on following Him.
- I will allow Him to conquer every part of my life, even the areas I would rather keep to myself.
- I will take Him at His word and trust Him when my feelings tell me otherwise.
- I will pray and ask God to show me what distractions repeatedly show up in my life.
- I will ask for His strength and wisdom to take care of these distractions.
- I understand that living a focused, abiding life will not always be easy, and so I will ask God for endurance to run my life's race and to finish strong.
- I will remember that God honors inner beauty. I will resist the temptation to emphasize my outward appearance at the expense of my inner life.
- I will look to the Lord expectantly—counting on Him to take my offerings and do something great with them. I will apply faith to every time I speak, serve, pray, or love. I will do my part with faith, and then look up to Jesus and watch Him work.

Try This

- This week, eliminate media from your "diet." As much as possible, stay away from the TV and computer screen. Use the time to do something more meaningful.

- Make it a regular practice to fast. Buy a book on fasting and do it safely and wisely. Fasting will bring more clarity and focus to your life than you can imagine.

- Regularly take more time to rest in God's presence. Ten minutes of *focused rest* will do far more to rejuvenate you than two hours of TV!

- Read biographies on some of the spiritual greats who went before us, such as Watchman Nee, A.W. Tozer, Charles Finney, Andrew Murray, Hannah Whitall Smith, Thomas à Kempis, and E.M. Bounds.

- Spend extra time meditating and praying over small portions of Scripture. Allow the Word to do its work in your heart.

- Bring your thoughts back to God as soon as you realize they've wandered. Make it your pursuit to live in His presence as you walk here on earth (Psalm 116:9).

As we wrap up this section on our spiritual health, let's look at how a life out of balance affects our spiritual health.

Effects of Spiritual Imbalance

✓ *Too much output, not enough input (over-servers):* tired; tend to struggle with self-righteousness, no margin, and little grace; can be judgmental and often lose perspective; relationships often strained

✓ *Too much input, not enough output (over-resters):* unmotivated; lack vision and passion; can tend to be critical of how the "servers" are doing things; struggle with feeling disconnected

Balance Application

I hope by now we've eliminated many of the things that slow us down and have applied what we've known to do for so long but have failed to do. I pray by now you're walking through life more intently, more passionately, and more focused on the Lord and His calling on your life.

We now know what keeps us strong: nourishment, response, and rest. When we manage our physical and spiritual lives at this level, we will more easily maintain balance. We may have a busy week, but never again a busy "year." We may gain a few pounds, but never again three dress sizes. We may miss a quiet time or two, but never again a whole week. We will manage what God has given us with a much closer eye. We will keep the main things the main things. We will guard our intimacy with God. We will take good care of our loved ones. We will serve as God leads. We will get sufficient exercise. We will protect our times of rest. We will pursue a heart of peace.

Life is work. We might as well work at keeping our feet on the ground and our gaze fixed on heaven. As it says in 1 Timothy 4:8, godliness holds promise both in this life and the life to come.

Study Time

1. Read 2 Peter 1:2-4. Verse 2 is my prayer for you. Verse 3 and the first part of verse 4 speak of what we've been provided. What *has* He given us? The latter part of verse 4 tells us two reasons He has provided these things. Write them down.

2. Can we take hold of one without letting go of the other? Explain.

3. Read 2 Peter 1:5-7. Draw a vertical line. At the bottom, cross the vertical line with a short horizontal line. On that line write "faith." Just above faith, write the virtue this verse tells you to add to your faith. On top of that virtue, write the next one. There should be eight in all. Now look at your vertical line as a wall and look at the stacked virtues as bricks. When you build your life up with these things, you fortify it. Come back to this question when you have more time and really pray over these

"bricks." Ask God to increase your capacity for every one of them.

4. Read 2 Peter 1:8. Notice the "movement" referred to in this verse. We are called to grow. Based on this verse, what are the positive effects of possessing these qualities?

5. We send our kids to college so they will be equipped to make a living. We hold our kids accountable so they will grow in character. We laugh a lot with our kids so they won't take themselves too seriously. We love our kids immensely so they will more easily comprehend the love of Christ. This passage from 2 Peter tells us God has given us everything we need to live a life of power and godliness so we can participate in His divine nature and thus escape the corruption in the world. We are set up to thrive. The only remaining factor is our yes. Will you say yes to Him today? Will you trust Him with what stresses you out? Will you believe Him when He says He loves you? Will you follow wherever He leads? Please say yes.

And that about wraps it up. God is strong, and He wants you strong. Take everything the Master has set out for you—well-made weapons of the best materials—and put them to use so you can stand up to everything the devil throws your way. This is no afternoon athletic contest that we'll walk away from and forget about in a couple of hours. This is for keeps, a life-or-death fight to the finish against the devil and all his angels. Be prepared. You're up against far more than you can handle on your own. Take all the help you can get, every weapon God has issued, so that when it's all over but the shouting, you'll still be on your feet. Truth, righteousness, peace, faith, and salvation are more than words. Learn how to apply them. You'll need them throughout your life. God's Word is an indispensable weapon. In the same way, prayer is essential in this ongoing warfare. Pray hard and long. Pray for your brothers and sisters. Keep your eyes open. Keep one another's spirits up so that no one falls behind or drops out (Ephesians 6:10-18 MSG).

May we walk with the Lord with a new boldness, humility, and confidence. May we be highly attuned to His voice and be quick to obey Him. May others be so inspired by our fruit and our faith and our perspective that they look up to Jesus for themselves. And may the Lord use every storm, every trial, and every blessing in our lives to make us more like Him. Press on, in His name!

What Keeps You Grounded, Balanced?

In the ever-increasing stress and chaos of our world, for me, having a thriving walk with God is everything—being much with Jesus is critical. I saturate myself in His Word. I listen for His voice. I'm fervent in prayer.

—Paula

Notes

Chapter 5—Be Nourished

1. C.S. Lewis, *Readings for Meditation and Reflection* (New York, NY: HarperCollins, 1992), 35.
2. Fasting brings impurities to the surface. If you do end up fasting for more than a day, you'll notice a coating on your tongue and potentially an increase in body odor. Because your body isn't being asked to process all the foods you would normally be eating, it can give itself to the task of purifying your system. We all have toxins in our bodies, and fasting gives our bodies the chance to get rid of them. Some of those toxins will surface on the tongue. Brush regularly and rinse out your mouth. These effects will go away once you start eating again.

Chapter 7—Time to Move!

1. There are varying opinions today for how much time we need for proper conditioning, and even for fat-burning exercise (which differs for us individually based on our body composition and current fitness level). I suggest you consult your fitness professional for an accurate assessment.

Chapter 9—God Enjoys You

1. Bo Stern, *Ruthless: Knowing the God Who Fights for You* (Colorado Springs, CO: NavPress, 2014), 103.

Chapter 11—A Healthy Spiritual Diet

1. If you want an excellent book on fortifying your walls, read Beth Moore's book *When Godly People Do Ungodly Things* (Broadman and Holman Publishers).
2. A.W. Tozer, *The Pursuit of God* (Camp Hill, PA: Christian Publications, 1995), 151.

Chapter 12—A Healthy Thought Life

1. Catherine Marshall, *Something More* (Grand Rapids, MI: Chosen Books, 1974), 148.

Chapter 13—Spiritual Strength and Endurance

1. Oswald Chambers, *My Utmost for His Highest* (Grand Rapids, MI: Discovery House, 1992), November 18.

Chapter 14—Spiritual "Cardio"

1. Chip Ingram, *The Real Heaven* (Grand Rapids, MI: Baker Books, 2016), 77.
2. Marshall, *Something More*, 153.
3. Frances J. Roberts, *Come Away My Beloved* (Ojai, CA: King's Farspan, Inc., 1970), 56.
4. Rick Joyner, *There Were Two Trees in the Garden* (New Kensington, PA: Whitaker House/Morning Star Publications, 1993), 143–44.
5. Chambers, *My Utmost for His Highest*, May 25.

Chapter 15—What Words Do

1. Tozer, *The Pursuit of God*, 175–76.

Acknowledgments

Special and heartfelt thanks:

To Steve Laube, my wonderful agent—I appreciate you so very much.

To Leslie Wilson, my friend and helpful editor—Thank you for your friendship and support, and for sharing your expertise with me.

To Dr. Kristi Haertl, former fitness colleague—Thank you for sharing your valuable insights and advice. You are such a pro!

To LaRae Weikert, Betty Fletcher, and the Harvest House team—You're all so wonderful. I'm thrilled you decided to re-release this book. Thank you.

To my Facebook friends—Thank you for sharing from your valuable personal experiences. I know our readers will benefit from your hard-earned wisdom.

To my husband, three sons, and daughters-in-love—What can I say that I've not already said? You're my happy place, my treasured possession, and the delight of my heart. Love you all so much.

To Jesus—After all these years of walking with You, the awe is still not lost on me. I marvel at Your goodness and Your grace. And I can't wait to see You face-to-face. Blessed be Your Name forever!

About the Author

Susie Larson is a talk radio host, national speaker, and author of 15 books and many articles. Susie has been married to her dear husband, Kevin, since 1985, and together they have three wonderful sons, three beautiful daughters-in-law, and one adorable pit bull named Memphis. Susie's passion is to see women everywhere awakened to the value of their soul, the depth of God's love, and the height of their calling in Christ Jesus.

Susie worked in the fitness industry off and on for approximately 15 years. Certified for many years by the American Council on Exercise, Susie also worked as a fitness trainer for the National Exercise Trainers Association (formerly known as NDEITA) and as the group fitness coordinator for several health club systems, including Life Time Fitness.

Connect with Susie:
Web: www.susielarson.com
Facebook: www.facebook.com/deeperlifeinChrist
Twitter: @SusieLarson
Susie's Radio Show: *Live the Promise*: http://myfaithradio.com/
programs/live-the-promise/

Or by e-mail at: info@susielarson.com

To learn more about Harvest House books and
to read sample chapters, visit our website:

www.harvesthousepublishers.com

HARVEST HOUSE PUBLISHERS
EUGENE, OREGON